MW00466616

"My fear and cry for hel... year of counseling I continue to grow and become ... I wanted to be all along. He helped me understand I'm not a bad person, I just made bad decisions. He opened the doors so I could forgive myself and heal."—*Suzie, Georgia*

"Thanks to Terry I was able to get a handle on my life. It wasn't easy. I had to revisit 50 years of my life: how-when-where-why? The light finally came on. I needed to like myself, take care of myself, and love myself. Now I do and everything has changed! I used to take care of everyone else first. I still share and care but I include myself now. When leaving a store now. I can say I had a successful day and mean it."—*S.K., Ontario, Canada*

"My work with Terry has been very enlightening! He guided me on a path of self-discovery and growth and offered the support I needed. Through 10 sessions with him, I learned many new skills for living with this addiction, had the chance to try them out and then got to share my experiences in my next session. I felt that together we built a solid base for my recovery and I highly recommend Mr. Shulman's counseling."—*T.C., Chicago*

"My willingness to change and Mr. Shulman's program have truly changed me. If I had known about this program earlier, I could have avoided so much pain, trouble and legal issues."—*A.C., New Orleans*

"I had a healing, cleansing experience by counseling with Mr. Shulman. He not only helped me understand why I had been stealing, but gave me the tools and the confidence to see the warning signs of future relapses."—*Dave, Virginia*

BOUGHT OUT AND $PENT!

RECOVERY from
COMPULSIVE $HOPPING and $PENDING

Terrence Daryl Shulman, JD, LMSW

Author of
SOMETHING FOR NOTHING:
Shoplifting Addiction and Recovery
and
BITING THE HAND THAT FEEDS:
The Employee Theft Epidemic...
New Perspectives, New Solutions

INFINITY
PUBLISHING.COM

Copyright © 2008 by Terrence Daryl Shulman

All rights reserved. No part of this book shall be reproduced or transmitted in any form or by any means, electronic, mechanical, magnetic, photographic including photocopying, recording or by any information storage and retrieval system, without prior written permission of the publisher. No patent liability is assumed with respect to the use of the information contained herein. Although every precaution has been taken in the preparation of this book, the publisher and author assume no responsibility for errors or omissions. Neither is any liability assumed for damages resulting from the use of the information contained herein.

ISBN 978-0-7414-4730-2

Published by:

PUBLISHING.COM

Info@buybooksontheweb.com
www.buybooksontheweb.com
Toll-free (877) BUY BOOK
Local Phone (610) 941-9999
Fax (610) 941-9959

Printed in the United States of America

Published November 2012

Dedication

I dedicate this book to the millions of people around this world who have struggled with money and who search for true abundance and healing. May this book serve as a lifeline to recovery. You are not alone. There is hope.

I also dedicate this book to the brave souls who have contributed their stories in this book and to my many clients who contribute to my learning, to those who have already sought help, and to those who have made a difference in the lives of others by seeing with curiosity, compassion and faith the pain and the hope in each other.

Table of Contents

PART FOUR
Related Issues

Acknowledgments

As with my first two books, there are so many people I wish to acknowledge. Please forgive me if I have forgotten any of you who have touched my life.

My beautiful & supportive wife, Tina,
My mother Madeline & my stepdad Jim,
My brothers Jordy, Sam, and Marty,
My nephew Devan,
My father, Robert, rest in peace,
All of my relatives for their unconditional love and support,

My best buddies who have kept me strong and centered: Lee Anzicek, Tom Lietaert, Dick Halloran, Brett Koon, Scott McWhinney, Rob Koliner, Joe Sulak, Dana L. Piper, Marty Peters, Ben Goryca, Kevin Lauderdale, Josh Barclay, Chuck Pavey, Andrew Miller, Michael Fox, Jeff Gabrielson and David McCurdy.

Steve Campbell, mentor and friend, rest in peace,

Dana L. Piper for back cover photograph,

Cathy Dyer, of Mandalas Awakening, for book cover design,

My Goddess cheerleading squad: Julie Brydon, Laura Hansen-Koon, Andrea Sulak, Sharon Harris, Bryn Fortune, Stacy Arsht-Fox, Mona Light, Robin Schwartz, Megan Powers, Carol Klawson, Amy Goldstein-McCurdy, Christina Pavey, Gigi Colombini, & Maureen McDonald,

Nancy Rabitoy of Better Direction Design,

Benji and Penelope, the love dogs,

My fellow recovering friends in C.A.S.A. (Detroit area),

My fellow recovering friends on C.A.S.A.'s e-mail group,

Secular Organization for Sobriety (S.O.S.), especially June F. (r.i.p.), Dale, Jim G. (r.i.p.), Tim, & Chuck,

Landmark Education Corporation,

Stan Dale (r.i.p.) and the angels of the Human Awareness Institute,

The Detroit Area Men's Wisdom Council,

The Tuesday morning men's breakfast club,

The Mankind Project,

Bert Whitehead & Carol Johnson

Dr. Eugene Ebner, PhD,

Dr. John Brownfain, PhD, rest in peace,

Elizabeth Corsale (Shoplifters Recovery Program),

Dr. Jon E. Grant,

John Prin of TrueYouRecovery

April Benson of www.stoppingovershopping.com,

Dr. Natasha Kendal and Pamela Landy, JD,CFP

Lyn Kelley, GROW Institute

Those who contributed their stories in this book, and

The folks at Infinity Publishing.

<u>Disclaimer</u>

The stories herein are composites of various clients I have worked with. Names and details have been changed to protect the anonymity and confidentiality of these persons.

About the Author

Terrence Daryl Shulman is a native Detroiter, an attorney, therapist, and consultant. He's been in recovery since 1990 and founded C.A.S.A. (Cleptomaniacs And Shoplifters Anonymous), a weekly support group, in 1992 in the Detroit area. C.A.S.A. is one of only a handful of groups of its kind.

He founded the website www.kleptomaniacsanonymous.com in 1999, www.employeetheftsolutions.com in 2003 and www.shopaholicsanonymous.org in 2004.

Mr. Shulman is the founder and director of The Shulman Center for Compulsive Theft & Spending. He specializes in counseling clients with theft addictions and disorders and/or compulsive shopping/spending. He works with clients both in person and by phone. Previously, he worked extensively as a chemical dependency counselor and was a clinic Director.

He has been featured on various television programs, notably Oprah, Prime Time Live, 48 Hours, Prime Time, Fox Files, Inside Edition, Extra!, Montel, The Today Show, The Early Show, Ricki Lake, Queen Latifah, CNN News, Fox Cable News, The Discovery Channel, Women's Entertainment TV, The Mike & Juliet Show and numerous local news programs.

He has been featured in various magazines and newspaper articles in The New York Times, The Chicago Tribune, The Detroit Free Press, The Detroit News, The Metro Times, Lifetime, Health, Redbook, Cosmopolitan, Good Housekeeping, TV Guide, Hour Magazine, O Magazine, Counselor Magazine, Addiction Professional, and The Psychotherapy Networker.

He organized the First International Conference on Theft Addictions and Disorders in Detroit in 2005 and the 2nd International Conference on Compulsive Theft & Spending in Detroit in 2008.

This is Mr. Shulman's third book.

Mr. Shulman lives in Southfield Michigan with his wife Tina.

Preface

We all have money issues. I know I do. We're usually feeling like we want or need more of it. We're trying to earn more, spend less, save or invest more; yet, we also want more, need more, feel we deserve more, and dread the feeling of losing or just maintaining our current lifestyle. Yet, money is also taboo—even more than sex. We talk openly about sex. But when was the last time we told a close family member or friend *exactly* how much we earn per year, how much we spend, how much we owe? Do we even know ourselves? Likely, we know just as little about the financial details of others who are close to us. Why is this?

I believe something else is happening. A dangerous mindset has taken root: spend now and worry later—or, better yet, don't worry at all! Welcome to the world of addiction: the world of more, more, more. It's a world of secrets, shame, imbalance, of denial, and insanity. It's more than plain greed.

You've probably noticed a growing trend over the last decade or so. From Suze Orman to Dave Ramsey to Oprah's "Debt Diet" to A&E TV's "Big Spender" to books, articles, television and radio shows: calls near and far are sounding the alarm about our individual and collective problems with debt and spending.

Everywhere we look and listen: there are warning signs that something is out of balance: a looming recession, wild stock market swings, a housing market bust with record foreclosures, and consumer credit card debt at an all time high!

We were given easy credit, no money down, and promised "The American Dream." Look what's happening?

As Americans, we work longer hours, take less vacation

time, have more health issues such as lack of sleep, depression, anxiety, and obesity, and report less overall satisfaction with life. As we continue to emulate and chase the lifestyles of the "rich and famous," we pay a devastating toll—individually and collectively.

Yet, many of us continue to spend like there's no tomorrow. And, for many, there may not be a tomorrow. Bankruptcies and suicides are rising, too, as many lose everything. These stories, however, are not as well-reported.

Mixed messages abound. After the 9/11 attacks, we were told by President Bush, "We cannot let the terrorists achieve the objective of frightening our nation to the point where we don't conduct business, where people don't shop…Mrs. Bush and I want to encourage Americans to go out shopping." We went shopping, all right, but our economy is still floundering. If we don't shop wisely, don't save, don't invest, and don't buy good health insurance and have enough left over for the kids' college and our own retirement—that's not good for the economy or us.

The U.S. economy went from a surplus in the 1990s to being $3 trillion in debt. Most states have balanced budget amendments which force them to correct any debt every two years. We could blame the national debt solely on the war in Iraq—certainly that's played a part. But there's more…

Our attitude and culture of consumerism have reached a breaking point over the last few decades. As global warming—through natural disasters and dying species—screams out for us to change our thinking and behavior, so do the financial signs of the times—through our own bank accounts. We're living beyond our means! And the rest of the world—especially China, India, and Russia—are fast following our lead.

As with many issues, we seem to have a split personality—

again, individually and collectively. On the one hand, we have a trend toward hyper-consumerism best illustrated by the blossoming of magazines and TV shows pushing the lure of haute couture and mocking—tongue-in-cheek—the excesses of shopping and spending—from "Sex in The City" to the chick-lit "Confessions of a Shopaholic" novellas which will be released as a major motion picture this year.

On the other hand, we have a growing movement saying slow down—from Suze Orman to the movies "What Would Jesus Buy?," "Maxed Out!," and the underground films "Money as Debt," Freedom to Fascism," and "Zeitgeist."

In 2006, a landmark Stanford University study concluded that something else may better describe the phenomenon that is growing among millions of people. It is called "compulsive buying disorder." While still controversial—there's a tendency to call it "poor money management"—it opens a new window towards prevention and treatment of persons whose buying and spending may not be helpable through conventional approaches such as just cutting up credit cards or trying to follow a financial advisor's counsel.

Consider the following statistics:

*17 Million Americans (roughly 6% of the population) are compulsive buyers (Stanford University Study, 2006)

*Nearly half of all compulsive buyers are men (Stanford University Study, 2006)

*Arguments over money and spending are the primary reason for couples' conflict or divorce (Psychology Today)

*The average credit card debt per American citizen is nearly $10,000—mostly from unnecessary purchases (Time and Money magazines)

This book isn't a book about finances from the viewpoint of how to make more money or how to save more money. It's more about our emotional and psychological relationship to money and to things. It's about going deeper—to the roots.

My interest in this subject is also personal. My own tendency is more toward a fear of shopping or spending which developed largely in reaction to witnessing my father's care-free spending and poor money management. This—along with his alcoholism—led to my parents' divorce when I was ten years old. Our family saw tough times and was on welfare for a while. I learned the value of "living on the minimum necessary." However, my grief, fear, and anger led me into shoplifting and employee theft over a ten year period through my mid-teens to mid-20s.

Since 1990, through my own recovery from addictive-compulsive stealing, I also have had to confront my own dysfunctional attitudes and patterns around money and spending. While I don't claim to have this mastered, I appreciate how far I've come. I've been fortunate to be debt-free, live in a modest home, drive a modest car, and share a modest but comfortable lifestyle with my wife. Everyday, I make choices about my money and my spending.

I have also enjoyed working as an addictions therapist since 1997 to help other people regain balance in all aspects of their lives. In working with recovering drug addicts, alcoholics, shoplifters, and people who steal from work, I've been amazed at the extent of money dysfunctions. Many people can't seem to generate enough income, they blow through money—often the product of their own addictions—or they make money a God, a magic pill that would solve all problems. And the debt!

I began to see how our relationship to money and things is a huge source of wounding and pain in my clients—and most people in general. Therefore, creating a new relationship with money and things can, equally, bring healing and peace.

Since 2004, I began counseling compulsive shoppers and spenders in addition to my primary work with people who compulsively steal. Often, both behaviors—compulsive theft and spending—are present either at the same time or at different stages.

My work is fascinating and rewarding. I continue to study and learn more about this field and have felt privileged to appear on numerous shows and programs which have highlighted this growing problem with shopping and spending.

I recall in 1993, when my father died, I was a newly practicing attorney and handled the administration of his estate—or what was left of it. He had continued to spend wildly even during the last several years of his life despite being in a wheelchair from a stroke. He left nearly $100,000 in debt and no life insurance or real property. Somehow, I was able to salvage a few thousand dollars for my stepmom, myself and my two younger brothers. That was another wake-up call. I opened a savings account on the dot, took out a life insurance plan at the age of 28, and vowed to do my best not to live or die with debt.

In the last several years, I have also watched one of my brother's exhibit compulsive shopping behavior. As a first-time father, he steadily began buying his young son more and more toys and games. Though he didn't seem to go in to debt over it, he had a modest income and a small apartment and, eventually, began running out of room. Seeing his son primarily on weekends, he never missed an opportunity to give his son a gift. At my nephew's birthday parties, each family member would show up with one gift; my brother literally had 20-30 gifts wrapped for him. It was a spectacle.

My primary worry was that my brother was overindulging and spoiling him. It was also clear to me that he was trying earnestly to show the love for his son that our father hadn't showed for us—even though our own father was prone to buying or spending to compensate for his other shortcomings. It seemed my brother had fallen into that trap as well. If anyone brought up a concern, my brother would get defensive, stating: "I just love to see my son smile."

Recently, however, my brother did begin to admit he was a compulsive shopper. In addition to feeling the burden of a crowded apartment, he began to see what he created. His son began to ask for more and more toys and would cry or sulk when he didn't get them. Further, as my nephew began to grow, his interests began to shift and my brother realized he was left with a mountain of useless toys and games. There were other complicated issues at hand, too—things that couldn't be made right by a new toy.

I'm reminded of the old saying: "you can't solve most issues with money or things." Most of us have experienced this lesson already. We see how "the rich and famous" still have problems. We've heard the stories of lottery winners who blow their money all too quickly, fall into depression or addictions, or who end up saying they wish they'd never won. Yet, we still buy into the fantasy that more money or more things will make us happy.

I hope this book is another offering among the many out there which helps us look at, understand better, and make the necessary changes in our lives so we may live our best lives possible.

Terrence Daryl Shulman,
Southfield, Michigan, March 2008

Introduction

Are You Bought Out and $pent?

If you're reading this book, either you or someone you know may have serious problems with shopping or spending. There are different ways to determine if there's really a problem. If you think there's a problem, usually there is. If others think you have a problem, usually there is. Ultimately, each one of us has to decide this for him/herself.

Sometimes there may be a problem with debt but not so much because of shopping—one may not shop regularly but may spend too much money on occasional larger purchases such as a home, a car, a vacation; or, one may spend too much on dining out, concerts, the theatre, etc. Likewise, one may have a compulsive shopping or spending problem but not be in debt—there may be other consequences like loss of time or interest in relationships, avoidance of emotions or of obligations.

Some common reasons why people over-shop or overspend include the following:

--Emotional and/or material deprivation in childhood
--Inability to tolerate negative feelings, pain, loneliness, depression, fear, or anger
--Need to fill an inner void—empty and longing inside
--Excitement or thrill-seeking
--Approval seeking
--Perfectionism
--Need to gain control
--Manic episodes, ADHD, or impulsivity

Compulsive shoppers—often referred to as "shopaholics" can sometimes be described in categories such as these:

*Trophy shoppers

*Image shoppers

*Bargain shoppers

*Codependent shoppers

*Bulimic shoppers

*Collector shoppers

*Compulsive shoppers

These categories will be fleshed out later. Whatever the reasons, whatever the labels or categories, problems with money, debt, buying, shopping or spending need to be taken seriously. The following are a few questionnaires designed to help determine if there is a problem with compulsive shopping or spending.

20 Question Assessment from The Shulman Center

1. Have you ever lost time from work or school due to shopping/spending?

2. Has shopping/spending ever created problems in your relationships?

3. Has shopping/spending ever affected your reputation or people's opinion of you?

4. Have you ever felt guilt, shame, or remorse after shopping/spending?

5. Did you ever shoplift or steal from work to get money to pay debts or to solve money issues?

6. Did shopping/spending ever cause a decrease in your ambition or efficiency?

7. Did you ever experience a "high" or "rush" of excitement when you shop or spend?

8. Have you ever shopped/spent to escape worries?

9. Has shopping/spending caused you to have difficulty eating or sleeping?

10. Do arguments, disappointments or frustrations create an urge to shop or spend?

11. Have you noticed you began shopping or spending more frequently over time?

12. Have you ever considered self-destruction or suicide as a result of your shopping/spending?

13. Upon stopping over-shopping or overspending did you continue to be tempted/preoccupied by it?

14. Have you kept your shopping/spending a secret from most of those you are close to?

15. Have you told yourself "this is my last time" and still over-shopped or overspent again?

16. Have you continued to shop or spend despite having been had legal issues such as bankruptcy or divorce?

17. Do you often feel angry or feel a need for control?

18. Do you often have feelings of life being unfair?

19. Do you have persistent feelings of entitlement to get or buy what you want?

20. Do you have trouble speaking up for yourself, asking for help, or saying "no"?

What was your score? How many times did you answer yes?

Most compulsive shoppers/spenders will answer <u>yes</u> to <u>at least seven (7)</u> of these questions. This questionnaire is adapted from the Gamblers Anonymous 20 Questions. Debtors Anonymous & professional counseling should be recommend for compulsive shoppers/spenders.

Another assessment tool—The Compulsive Buying Scale— by Valance, D'Astous & Fortier can be found on the website:

15 Questions of Debtors Anonymous

1. Are your debts making your home life unhappy?

2. Does the pressure of your debts distract you from your daily work?

3. Are your debts affecting your reputation?

4. Do your debts cause you to think less of yourself?

5. Have you ever given false information in order to obtain credit?

6. Have you ever made unrealistic promises to your creditors?

7. Does the pressure of your debts make you careless of the welfare of your family?

8. Do you ever fear that your employer, family or friends will learn the extent of your total indebtedness?

9. When faced with a difficult financial situation, does the prospect of borrowing give you an inordinate feeling of relief?

10. Does the pressure of your debts cause you to have difficulty sleeping?

11. Has the pressure of your debts ever caused you to consider getting drunk?

12. Have you ever borrowed money without giving adequate consideration to the rate of interest you are required to pay?

13. Do you usually expect a negative response when you are subject to a credit investigation?

14. Have you ever developed a strict regimen for paying off your debts, only to break it under pressure?

15. Do you justify your debts by telling yourself that you are superior to the "other" people, and when you get your "break" you'll be out of debt overnight?

How did you score? If you answered yes to eight or more of these questions, the chances are that you have a problem with compulsive debt, or are well on your way to having one. If this is the case, today can be a turning point in your life.

11 Questions of Shopaholics Anonymous

1. Do you "take off for the stores" when you've experienced a setback or a disappointment, or when you feel angry or scared?

2. Are your spending habits emotionally disturbing to you and have they created chaos in you life?

3. Do your shopping habits create conflicts between you and someone close to you (spouse, lover, parents, or children)?

4. Do you buy items with your credit cards that you wouldn't buy if you had to pay cash?

5. When you shop, do you feel a rush of euphoria mixed with feelings of anxiety?

6. Do you feel you're performing a dangerous, reckless or forbidden act when you shop?

7. When you return home after shopping, do you feel guilty, ashamed, embarrassed or confused?

8. Are many of your purchases seldom or never worn or used? Do you lie to your family or friends about what you buy and how much you spend?

9. Would you feel "lost" without credit cards?

10. Do you think about money excessively—how much you have, how much you owe, how much you wish you had—and then go out and shop again?

11. Do you spend a lot of time juggling accounts and bills to accommodate your shopping debts?

If you answered "yes" to any of these questions, it is wise to consider you may be headed for trouble. If you answered "yes" to more questions that you answered "no," it is wise for you to seek professional help immediately.

Go to www.shopaholicsanonymous.org

Also, a new, improved assessment scale is set to be released this year (2008). Keep checking our website for details...

So, are you *bought out and spent*? If not yet but getting there, stop before it's too late! If you already are, you can get your life back. Read on...

This book is divided into four parts:

Part One highlights stories of those I've worked with who have been compulsive shoppers or spenders: a human face on this problem.

Part Two provides a guide to various reasons why people over-shop or overspend and other money dysfunctions as well as important data, statistics, and the challenges and issues that arise.

Part Three includes exercises to help people stop over-shopping and overspending and move toward greater peace and wholeness in recovery

Part Four focuses on related topics which did not fit as well in the other parts.

Part One

A Human Face on Compulsive Shopping/ Spending

<u>Brad's Story</u>—The Collector Shopper

Brad, 38, is a reserved but playful young man. He lives alone and has been single all his life. A college graduate working in sales, Brad became a shopaholic at an early age. He woke up when he was fired from a job for employee theft—driven by the stress of mounting credit card debts.

My name is Brad and I'm a recovering shopaholic. It wasn't until I was fired and prosecuted for employee theft this year that I realized I had a problem. I had never done anything like that in my life and it was probably brought on because I was in such dire straights financially. I was struggling with my job. *But being in debt most of my adult life by over-shopping and overspending led me to cross a line I never thought I'd cross.* Being in debt isn't a crime—it's a sad situation—but stealing and committing a felony was what got my attention to seek help for the underlying issues.

I think my over-shopping and overspending were related to my parents divorce. I'm an only child but I have two step-brothers and two half-brothers. My parents got divorced when I was in 4th grade. I was about 10. I had a hard time with that—as I think any kid at that age would. I lived with my Mom and didn't want to see my Dad who got married so quickly after the divorce. I felt it was like a stigma. It drove a wedge between my relationship with my Dad and stepmom.

I developed this loner existence. I had friends but I also didn't keep in touch with some good friends in high school and college. I moved around a lot for college and jobs and there were 6 years where I was pretty much by myself.

1

The irony is—after college—I felt pretty good about myself at the time. I was the first of my friends to get out on my own, to get a job. My friends would visit me and say "hey, he's got his own apartment." *If I wanted something I would buy it. I felt I deserved it.* I had a lot of free time on my hands so I'd spend that time shopping. I'd go to the Mall, go to the movies, go to the CD store—this was all before DVD's. DVD's were my biggest pitfall. I had a huge cassette tape collection and then I had to transfer them onto CD's or buy new CD's; with VHS tapes, I had to go and buy all my favorite movies all over again on DVD. *I had this collector mentality and nobody seemed to think to correct my wrongs or challenge me about it. So, I felt, hey, I'm doing well on my own so I owe it to myself.*

I knew I had a problem with shopping and spending but I never let myself see that too clearly. My Mom kind of suspected it. It's funny because my folks were divorced when I was real young and my Dad always used to say that my Mom was a spendthrift. I don't want to blame my Mom but, obviously, I got some of this behavior from her; I was raised by her and went shopping often with her. I was the kind of kid who didn't mind going shopping.

I enjoyed shopping and, yet, I kind of kept it quiet. I didn't talk a lot about it with my friends. They must have suspected something was off, though. They knew I had a decent job but they'd make remarks because I'd have new clothes every week, new shoes, movies. They'd ask: "hey Brad, did you get the new CD or DVD?" And I'd always say "yes." And, you know, friends never tell friends how much money they really make. So, it seems to me they had to know something—I had too much stuff!

I remember this incident when I was a sophomore in high school. My Mom treated me and a buddy to a weekend at The Grand Traverse Resort on Christmas vacation. We swam in the pool and played in the game room. It was a blast! On the last day, my Mom took us to a music store and there was this cassette tape I wanted by Steven Wright—the comedian. I loved his stuff and used to imitate him for family and friends. That was fun. Anyway, I really wanted his cassette tape and asked my Mom to buy it for me. She told me "not right now, Christmas is just around the corner—maybe you'll get it then." I got so upset and, I'm embarrassed to say, threw this temper tantrum right in the store. I left the store and just sulked in the front seat of the car all the way home. I didn't talk to my Mom or even my friend.

When we got home, I threw my bags on the floor and was just acting like a brat. My Mom came into the room and she had something in her hand. She came toward me and said "I told you: be patient." Then she showed me the cassette I had wanted her to buy. But she said "this is what you were going to get for Christmas but you couldn't wait so now you're not going to get it at all." And then she placed it on the floor and took a hammer and smashed it into about ten pieces and made me clean it up. I think she started crying and then went to bed. The next morning we hardly talked to each other. To be quite honest, there were other occasions where I behaved the same way. *I was a brat. I just wanted what I wanted and this caused stress between me and my Mom. I think this was a warning sign that I needed help or at least needed to learn how not to be a jerk.*

After this event, though, I did get the picture that I should be more careful what I asked for, so I stopped asking for as much. That event with the hammer has really stuck with me—it's not the kind of thing that leaves easily. I definitely saw a behavioral shift in myself—maybe that's what my Mom wanted. Out of everybody, my Mom tried to help me the most. She even helped me with money to pay off my bills because she knew I was stressing at times. *She kind of enabled me in that regard. I feel like I've never really fully supported myself. I feel like I got into this awful routine where the only way I'd be happy is buying stuff.*

3

Several years later—about 5 years ago—my Mom had some serious health issues. I'm surprised this didn't come up in our therapy earlier. She had a condition where her brain's synapses were firing non-stop and her face was red all the time. She had to have brain surgery where they put gauze in her brain to interrupt the synapses from firing—that's as close as I can get to describing it.

I was in retail sales at the time—working as a shoe salesman at Neiman Marcus in the Mall. She and her boyfriend had moved to Chicago and her boyfriend suggested I come out on a weekend to see her before her surgery. I usually worked weekends but managed to get some time off. My intention was to go spend some time with my Mom because her surgery had already been postponed and she was really stressed. I was stressed, too, because I was in debt and having trouble paying my bills. I was virtually broke. I feel bad because instead of being there to support my Mom I ended up unloading on her about my money situation, how I didn't even have money for parking.

When I got back home I felt terrible. This isn't the kind of thing you want to throw at your Mom on the eve of surgery. She was in tears. *It was one of the worst moments of my life.* I hardly connected at all. When I left I said "good luck" but it was a very weak send-off. She ended up writing me a letter after her surgery basically forgiving me and letting me off the hook because of the stress we were both going though. I feel like I still need to apologize to her.

This feeling of guilt I have is prevalent—over the visit before her surgery, over the hammer and the cassette incident, even over my parents' divorce. I think I've blamed myself. There's also a lot of denial. I'd slough my spending off—and the guilt I felt afterwards—as just "buyer's remorse." I didn't know I was feeling guilty about other things, too. I was so stressed, though. Sometimes I'd be up at four in the morning with my calculator trying to figure out how I was going to pay my bills. I did the whole "borrowing from Peter to pay Paul" thing with my credit cards.

I look back on my years in high school and college and I feel I should have been more social. *It was kind of pathetic but it got to the point that the only time I was happy was when I was buying myself something. Sometimes I'd wait a bit before buying something so it would feel that much better when I did eventually buy it.* There were times I passed up going out with friends to go shopping instead or, if I didn't want to be out late, I'd leave early so I could get up in the morning to hit the stores. They never knew that. There were times I'd show up late for a party and have a trunk full of stuff and they didn't know that. *I was living a secret life.*

Eventually, my secret life came to an end...

I'd been working at Neiman Marcus for 8 years and I had tired of the job and my sales were falling off at times. Then in October 2006 I had this big trip to Chicago planned with some of my family members. I had no money and no way to pay for this trip. I couldn't even take a cash advance on my credit cards. What little money I had in my bank accounts had to stay in there for rent and car payments.

Then a little light bulb went off in my head: I'm around cash all the time, especially this time of year with the holidays coming—how easy would it be?—and I just had a big sale the night before with a $1,000 cash deal. A seed was planted. And then I had two large cash sales which came to about $800—which was just the amount I needed for the trip. And I told myself—if it happens—I'll take the opportunity and if it doesn't, I will cancel the trip or just ask somebody for a loan. But, fortunately—or unfortunately—I got those sales, voided them out on the register, and slipped the money in an envelope and put it in my duffle bag.

So, I was able to go on my trip and have a little left over to pay a few bills. The tough part was that we drove to Chicago from Detroit so I had a few hours to think about my actions. I weighed the pros and cons and it seemed that the pros outweighed the cons in my mind. I guess I was in denial. I rationalized it. I deserved the money. I should have had a better week than I had. I'm not hurting the company—which was a lie. It basically became a crime of convenience or, even, necessity.

The way I looked at it was I wasn't taking money to go blow at the casinos or on entertainment or at bars—most of it, eventually, went to pay bills. *I was stealing to help myself get out of debt. But what I was doing—and I didn't realize this at the time—was feeding my habit. If I didn't have this compulsion for overspending over the last several years I wouldn't have put myself in the position I was in.* I just put my blinders on and rationalized it to the point where it made sense and forgo the consequences.

It all went down on March 26, 2007. I went into work and at the end of the night the loss prevention manager called me into his office. His assistant was in there, too, and I knew right away they had me. I proceeded to sit there for about 3 hours and just answered their questions. Basically, they told me they had me on tape pocketing money at the cash register. Apparently, they just had someone come in at the end of my shift that night and pay in cash to see if I'd pocket it. It was $300 for a pair of shoes. Ironically, I almost didn't do it. It was the end of the night and I had already had a good night selling and didn't really need the extra money and just wanted to close and get out of the store. I could have just put the money in the drawer and closed out the shift.

I was arrested on the spot. It was the worst day of my life, easily. At the time it wasn't because it didn't feel like it was happening to me. I felt the bright lights on me. The phone call I made to my Mom was tough. At first, she thought I was joking. I told her it wasn't a joke. I've never joked about anything like that in my life. *The irony was that I hated thieves and here I became one.* Then she called my father because I didn't have the brass to call him myself.

I spent the night in jail. The next morning, I walked into court handcuffed and my Dad was there with a lawyer he had hired. *I couldn't even look my Dad in the eye.* I stood up before the judge and was released pending my next court date. I stayed with my Dad over the next few days because he wanted to talk to me. He couldn't get his hands around what I'd done and why I'd done it. Then my Dad, my Mom, her boyfriend, my stepmother had an intervention with me.

The following day I got a check in the mail from Neiman Marcus for $2,300. I think it was vacation pay and commissions owed to me. The next thing I knew, I spent $500 of it at the stores. My Dad hit the roof! He took away my debit card for the next few months and got me set up with online banking so he could monitor my spending. Even then, I overspent periodically. He couldn't believe it.

Coincidentally, my stepmother had just come across an article in the paper for The Shulman Center and thought it was on topic with what I was going through. I went online and checked out the websites and the information seemed to zero in on some of my behavioral patterns. I called Mr. Shulman and left a message. He called me back and we had about a half hour conversation to get some background and then set up a first meeting. Then I went back to Mr. Shulman's website and re-took the test to see if I was a compulsive shopper and I was stunned to see I met all the criteria. It was good because it helped my Dad understand that I really did have a problem. He was getting frustrated and taking it out on me but I think he began to understand.

Both of my parents have been really great throughout all this. I don't know if they've completely forgiven me but they seem to have come to terms with what I've done. I've always been close to my Mom but I've made great strides with my Dad through this. I'm still much more open with my Mom and I think that's the way it's always going to be—I don't think there's anything wrong with that. My Dad has been more forthcoming about inviting me to family gatherings. *We always used to just talk about sports but now he wants to hear how I'm really doing, how my recovery is going.* My Dad came to 2 therapy sessions with me—one with my Mom and me and one just with me.

I think I stole a total of twenty-two times over the period of October 2006 to March 2007. The total—according to loss prevention—was $8,500.00. The court costs, restitution, attorney, therapist—everything ended up costing about $15,000.00. So, all in all, I paid about double what I stole.

I began attending the C.A.S.A. (Cleptomaniacs And Shoplifters Anonymous) support group and have found it very helpful even though I was reluctant to attend at first. I think I didn't want to admit to anybody else what I had done—stolen. But after my first meeting, I think I've come to every meeting over the last 6 months except a few. It's been very good for me especially since I'm not in therapy anymore—it's good to go once a week. It's a constant reminder—about stealing and shopping—and at first I thought that was a negative but now I see that's a positive.

I've had people in the group tell me they've seen me grow or that they've seen a different side of me which I think is great. I don't go to group fishing for compliments because there are a lot of people there worse off than I am. I go there and it helps me stay grounded. It feels good to help other people, too. I've stayed after the group and talked to a few people. *I'm usually the one who doesn't talk much, rock the boat, or go outside his comfort zone, but I'm learning to do so.* It's been very significant. I've also taken a bit of a leadership role with 3 or 4 other group members and I look forward to continuing that.

I think I'm doing all right in recovery. I haven't stolen anything since my arrest and—as far as shopping and spending—I've bought a few small items but am keeping an eye on it. One of the things with my current sales work that is challenging is that I have a set schedule from 8am – 5pm Monday through Friday so I have a lot of down-time at night and on the weekends. My office is just a half mile from the Mall. I had temptations when I used to work at Neiman Marcus which was in the Mall. I still have some triggers—like when I have a bad day or I lose a sale—my first thought is: what can I do to make myself feel better? Buy a DVD! But, instead, I've been calling my Mom or a friend and just saying "I'm having a bad day" or I'll talk about football.

Yesterday I was really sad after watching a documentary on TV about PETA and animal rights. I told myself: "don't watch it—it'll make you feel bad." And it did. But I called my Mom and talked to her about it and told her maybe I should get involved in animal rights—something to put my energy toward—and she thought it was a great idea. So, there are things like that where I'm trying to curb these urges. Football season right now is really hard. I'd like to have these jerseys or those caps. I tell myself: I don't really need it. I've occasionally bought a CD or a DVD but I've managed to use gift certificates or to trade in used ones for new ones so I'm not breaking the bank so to speak. I'm doing the best I can. *The best thing is to stay out of stores.* I think from where I came from to now—I'm pretty happy.

My new job is stressful and next month I will have to make my first quota. I'm nervous but this is life. I'm learning to approach things differently. My family and friends have even told me they've seen me as less cynical and sarcastic which, I guess, is good. I just have to take it one day at a time as they say. I don't know what the future holds but at least I feel more hopeful about it these days.

Lately, I've been reconnecting with friends and deepening

my current friendships. I even attended my 20th High School reunion this year—which was really a coup for me. *I'm learning to step outside my box and put my energies into something I'm not used to doing. This has been helping me avoid shopping.*

Do I still have temptations? Yeah, and some days are better than others. But I find if I channel those thoughts and urges into something productive I'm all right—even if it's just sitting on the couch for 3 hours watching TV rather than going out shopping—that's a moderate success right there. I think as I get more involved with others that will help, too.

I've also thought about why I've never been in a serious romantic relationship. I think it has to do with how isolated I'd become. I get into this routine where it's all about me and what I want to buy or spend money on. I imagine it would be hard to adjust to buying things for another person, too. I've gotten kind of selfish. I'd have to change my lifestyle if I were in a relationship. I'm interested in being in a relationship one day but I've still got my routines. My Mom would like to see me with somebody, too, but we both know I need to be cautious and just get my life on track for a while yet. Right now, with my current job, I'm still living paycheck to paycheck.

Sometimes I wonder if I'm not shopping now because I just can't afford to. Will the test come when I'm actually making more money? I'm expecting a few commission checks soon and I'm wondering how I'll respond. I feel confident I will do okay. If I don't, at least there's no hiding it anymore.

Update: *Brad made his sales quota but was eventually let go from his job but is seeking new employment. He has paid off his debts, is saving money, continues to attend C.A.S.A. meetings and has his shopping and spending in check.*

Notes & Reflections:

Dollie's Story—The Bulimic Shopper

Dollie, 50, is a recovering alcoholic, overeater, shopaholic and shoplifter. A middle-school teacher, Dollie is fragile and child-like at times. Her father and a close friend died recently which triggered shopping and shoplifting binges.

Dollie came to see me shortly after being arrested for shoplifting. She stated from the outset that her main problem was over-shopping and overspending. She had a pattern of buying and exchanging or returning—mostly clothing. She described herself as a recovering food addict. She also has been a recovering alcoholic for 24 years. Dollie was very fearful of her job finding out about her shoplifting arrest as she feared being fired.

Dollie's father was an alcoholic and drug addict. She had been in counseling four different times over a 13-year period but had never addressed her compulsive shopping and spending. *"My Mom made me go shopping with her. My Mom made me her confidant which made me feel helpless."*

Dollie's life took a turn two years ago when a good friend of hers in A.A. died suddenly. This man's father had been sexually inappropriate with her. *"After his death I started shopping excessively and overspending. Shopping is like a drug.* Then I started to take things back. The store clerks would get mad at me, so I guess I started to shoplift instead."

Dollie's father was physically and emotionally abusive toward her. She also suffered beatings from a man she was with during her early recovery in A.A. She was married for 5 years. She described her husband as "nice but hollow." She started teaching around the time she was married but put her interests in art and violin on the back burner. "I felt like a failure." Her paternal grandfather sexually abused her from age 3-8. She kept this secret until age 12 when she told her parents but they bought a house with him. She felt betrayed.

"I did confront my grandfather when I was 24. First he denied it but then he said 'I'm sorry I hurt you.' It felt icky. I've been depressed since 16. Even with all my therapy I still don't feel like I've healed much."

That's because you've alternated medicating your pain with alcohol, shopping, shoplifting, eating and caretaking others, I suggested to her.

"My father died recently. My Dad set the bar high. He wouldn't let us win. He kept raising the bar. I'm so tired. Now I have to take care of my Mom and she demeans me."

You're a good candidate for Alanon, I said. I also saw a pattern of procrastination and perfectionism in her.

Dollie went to local C.A.S.A. (Cleptomaniacs And Shoplifters Anoymous) meetings and could relate to talk about shopping and shoplifting. She determined she needed to avoid stores and to create a budget; doing these things, however, proved somewhat difficult for her.

"My Mom and family don't know about my over-shopping and certainly not about my shoplifting. *I'm keeping this a secret. I'm afraid of disappointing them."* Dollie also shared that when she was a little girl she observed her Mom shoplift. "I'm caretaking my Mom. She's undiagnosed as anorexic and I'm overweight. I'm the opposite: I've rebelled. I'm scheduled for lap-band surgery on my stomach."

"I have to learn to speak up. I'm not a victim." Dollie knew her deep fear of connecting with others. "Teaching in elementary school, the kids would hug me. Then, this year, I got moved to middle school—the kids are less friendly."

We worked on some concrete positive goals. Debbie cleaned out a closet and also had a heart to heart with her brother.

"I have this conflict inside of me. I have to deny myself anything good, yet, I need something. There's a void. Then I give in to shopping and stealing. What I really need is comfort, affection, trust, a sense of worth and balance."

Toward the end of our treatment, Dollie shared with me that she broke down and cried at work in front of some of her co-workers. "I had a 'grief bomb' over my Dad's death. Something triggered it." The ice was beginning to thaw. She was coming back into her emotional body.

However, not too surprisingly, she soon went shopping at Kohl's department store. "I set a limit of $100 and spent $150. I had no real temptations to steal, though." Again, Dollie minimized the problem. I strongly suggested she join a grief and loss support group.

I also discovered that Dollie had some other life goals: "I could write a children's book and illustrate it. I've had this idea for 10-15 years. I want to work on not overeating and not caretaking my Mom. If she wants something, I don't need to come running." I suggested Overeaters Anonymous and, again, Alanon or Co-Dependents Anonymous meetings.

Dollie took a trip to Flordia. "I shopped a bit more. I still feel disconnected. I've been missing meetings but I feel I can shop at times without buying anything. I'm not too worried."

It was clear to me that Dollie was slipping back into denial. She was on the cusp of turning 50 and began to focus more on getting lap-band surgery to lose weight than her overall recovery. We had set up a session before her surgery which she cancelled. She did call me to let me know the surgery went well but I haven't heard from her since.

Notes & Reflections:

<u>Bobbie's Story</u>—The Co-Dependent Shopper

Bobbie is a dynamic Southern woman in her late sixties who just came to terms with her compulsive shopping & spending problems. She has been dealing with loss issues and is finally talking about her life in her first time in therapy.

Bobbie had been a shopper since she was a kid. "*My Mom taught me how to shop. I was spoiled and given everything. She bought things for other people as well.* My Dad was a doctor and was gone a lot. My Mom was lonely. I'm lonely, too. *When I shop, I tend to shop to give to others. But I always seem to get used and taken advantage of.* Even my own brother is stealing money from our parents' estate."

Bobbie is a successful businesswoman in the twilight of her career. She lives in a very well-to-do area of the country. She was divorced about 20 years ago and has never had children. She's battled several health issues but has never been in counseling or on any psychiatric medications. She sought me out during a time of mounting crises.

"It's been one thing after another over the last few years. In 1999, I had an immune breakdown. I'd been taking care of my mother for a few years at that point. I was hospitalized for several months. My business started to go down hill from there—being absent—and with the economy taking a downturn. Then my Mom died in 2001—that was devastating. She was like my best friend. Then my Dad died in 2004. I got no help from my younger brother with anything. He hasn't worked a day in his life.

"My property taxes have gone up and my work gone has gone down. I'm a workaholic, I admit it. *I've always been a spender but I've got to stop it. I can't seem to resist buying things for people—even those I don't care for. I'm gonna wind up in the poorhouse.* Now I'm mostly homebound due to my health. All I have is my dog."

It was clear Bobbie felt much the way her mother felt: lonely and neglected. In her heyday, Bobbie related how she was an accomplished athlete and quite the head-turner. "But I don't have time to be sad or sorry." Or so she told herself. It was clear that she was struggling to come to terms with aging, her bad knees, her declining health, and her fading beauty. "I'm not suicidal but it would be a relief to go," she proclaimed. It was as if she had nothing left to live for really.

Bobbie's relationships were very tenuous. "I've had a lot of girlfriends over the years but they have done me in with jealousy. I'm very skeptical of people—women especially; most of my friends are men. I trust people and then they shit on me. People have always tricked me as far back as high school. A lot of my employees have stolen from me. I have stopped hiring people who steal from me."

And yet, you find yourself constantly buying and giving to people. Why? I asked. "I don't know. That's part of what I hope you'll help me figure out. *I have a hunch I might actually be a needy person.*"

Bobbie shared how she started her business relatively late in life—about 20 years ago just around the time of her divorce. She ended up having several employees who she ended up taking care of. *"I've always tried to make everyone my friend."* Where do you think this come from? I asked.

"My father was an amazing man and my mother was the gentlest woman I ever knew. She was beautiful and talented but lonely. My father was a top surgeon. He was like God. But he was gone a lot. I might see my Dad for a few seconds a day—it seemed like an equal trade. But we had to be

17

perfect as kids. We had to be dressed a certain way. You played the piano when the Nuns came by. You had to make everyone like you. I always had an agenda or was on a mission.

"But everything came to a head about 20 years ago—around the time of my divorce and my starting my own business. My Mom had cancer and my Dad wasn't there for her. I hated him for it. And I just feel guilty about his recent death because I was still grieving my mother's death three years earlier and trying to heal myself as well." Tears flowed freely as Bobbie let go.

"I tried to take care of everyone. I bought things for everyone. I tried hard to be God. And, yet, when I was in the hospital, nobody was there for me. I guess I don't count. I realize: I don't count. The only place I feel I count is with my clients. They love me, and they pay me. I walk away from other people."

So, how do you feel this all relates to shopping and buying things for others? I asked

"I don't know. I'm one of those people who just shops impulsively. I have to get a channel lock on the Home Shopping Network. Someone once said: 'you just like to spend money.' I guess I just want people to like me."

You said it earlier, I said. You don't count. Maybe you count if you can give enough so that people like you.

"Is it really that simple?" Bobbie asked. I don't know if it's that simple; there's usually more.

"I am uncomfortable receiving from others and, yet, I get angry when I'm overlooked," she confessed. "Even my top employee has never invited me over to see her house. I miss my parents terribly. There's a big hole in my life. I was thinking of volunteering at Hospice but I can't help anybody

now. I need the help. I think I got a lot of issues from my mother. I don't feel love. I want to be on top so nobody will hurt me. But I am hurt. People don't think I have feelings. *You get to a point where you're not going to give anymore. Yet, life is lonely without giving.* You can't just shut down because people aren't who you want them to be."

It seems like you have this dilemma, I told her. On the one hand, people feel untrustworthy and needy and they seem to let you down; yet, you're lonely.

"But if I go to the store and get attention from the store personnel—it's like a B12 shot. It's safer to shop and be around people in that environment. Everyone is nice to me."

The phone rings during one of our sessions. It's Bobbie's fax line. *"It's my business manager faxing me my end of the month American Express statement. I hate this feeling—it's in the pit of my stomach.*

"Really, if I could have my way, I'd quit this job, this lifestyle, and move out of state. I'm still waiting for my parents' estate to settle. I want to leave this all behind and have a simple life and walk and fly fish and have a lake, mountains and log cabin in a small town, me and my dog. I want peace. I don't want anyone around me. I could work in the garden. People say: 'I don't know how to start a new lifestyle'—that's silly, you just start over. *I don't have a husband, lover, or child to consider... maybe I'm filling the void of not having these relationships."*

Wherever you go, there you are, I suggested. It was time to get busy interrupting the various patterns in Bobbie's life that were dragging her down. Just as with an alcoholic stopping drinking, or an overeater overeating, it was imperative for her to get a handle on her shopping and spending before anything else.

Besides our weekly counseling and accountability sessions, I gave Bobbie several assignments. I told her to consider closing or suspending her American Express account. I had her focus on her own health and to stay close to home to rest and self-nurture through other means than buying: lay by the pool, read, cook a meal, and listen to music. I told her if there were any events where she felt inclined to buy a gift, to just send a nice card instead. I also supported her choice let her membership lapse to a high-priced spa and social club which she hardly used.

Within a few weeks, Bobbie reported making real progress and feeling empowered, free, and confident for the first time in a long time. "I have to go in for surgery next week," she said. I won't be able to talk for a few weeks. After my surgery, I have a nurse coming to my home for two days and then an old friend is coming to live with me for a month."

Maybe this was Bobbie's ideal opportunity for some down time and to allow herself to be taken care of. A few weeks later, we continued our therapy. Bobbie's surgery was successful and she sounded upbeat. "Only 3 or 4 people knew about my surgery, but they all sent me gifts, cards, and flowers! I wrote thank you cards and, I admit, I felt very uneasy, though. This one woman who visited me has a mother who is ill—I felt like I didn't deserve it.

"This old friend of mine is here taking care of me—he's wonderful. I'm paying him and he's getting room and board but it's good for both of us. He's one of the few people I trust. He's got relatively little in life. All my rich friends are suspicious of him." Bobbie began to cry.

"I've really been hurt. We live in a crazy world. I think I have ulterior motives to giving. My mother was so good at everything. She was an amazing baker. She made date cakes around the holidays for everyone. She would give them to everybody all year long. *But, again, her giving was a sign*

she was in pain and lonely. She did everything to excess—
she was either very dirty or very clean. She always had to be
out doing something. Before she died I hadn't cared about
baking but during the first year after she died I baked over
300 cakes and took them to work, nursing home, neighbors.

"I think my father and his parents made her lonely. He was
supposed to marry a very wealthy girl. My Mom was from a
good family but not wealthy. I caught my Dad at age 20
having an affair and was upset and confronted him but he
told me if I told her they'd get a divorce and he'd never talk
to me again. *I kept it a secret.* I feel like I loved my Dad
more than my Mom even though I also hated him. I feel like
my Mom was sick for so long I should have done more for
her." More tears…

It's as if Bobbie was keeping her mother's spirit alive by
continuing to shop and give gifts to others as she had done.
Some of Bobbie's fondest memories were of spending time
with her mother shopping. She studied her mother's ways
and admired them while knowing on some deep level her
shopping could not cure her loneliness. Bobbie found herself
repeating the same cycle; yet, she felt trapped, addicted. To
stop shopping and giving to others would take not only a
strong effort to change the pattern itself but would remove
the primary salve for all her other underlying feelings.
Besides, she'd go through a protracted period of feeling an
immense amount of guilt by stopping her giving. But, it's
what she knew she must do.

She had stumbles and starts and caught herself when she'd
relapse and "brush herself off" and start over again. She had
to resist the game she found herself in within her high
society. *"People talk, you know? Ever since I quit the spa
and social club, people are thinking I must be broke. But,
frankly, I don't care. Let them talk. I didn't want to play that
game anyway."*

It was as if Bobbie had been living this high lifestyle, at least in part, for her mother who came from humble origins and who never quite fit in with the jet-setters. But neither did Bobbie.

"I'm realizing I'm not very good with boundaries," she said. "My business partner fell down and broke her arm and I went on a bit of shopping binge and bought her something for about $160. I could have just gotten a card. *I mean, I love to make people happy giving them special gifts—but it ends up feeling like I'm giving away too much. Interestingly, I have received a few gifts from others lately. I actually felt like I could receive them and felt they were sincere."*

Bobbie and I continued to work on having her avoid certain stores and the Mall. She continued to feel more confident and hopeful about herself and excited about the changes she was making. She had streamlined her life to a small circle of friends who she basically trusted. They had monthly gatherings—typically at her home—but she asked for help in hosting at their homes and also asked others to help her when she was hosting. For her, these were baby steps and big steps at the same time.

Her next real challenge was to confront her brother who had been stealing from their deceased parents' estate. She was working with a lawyer and was frustrated with him. She was in the process of hiring a new lawyer when she abruptly discontinued therapy. I haven't heard from her since. I feel confident, however, that her first endeavor into therapy was productive. I feel it helped her clarify her feelings, her patterns, what was driving her shopping and spending, and what tools to use and changes to embrace to live an empowered life.

So the journey goes. One day at a time...

Notes & Reflections:

<u>Robert's Story</u>—The Compulsive/Image Shopper

Robert is a 50-year old professional man who was on the brink of suicide, divorce, and financial ruin due to his compulsive shopping and shoplifting.

Robert came to me as a referral from a local psychiatrist. He recently had been arrested for shoplifting but it soon became clear he also struggled with chronic over-shopping and overspending. He was on his second marriage and had a young son, 10, with his current wife. He had been in Alcoholics Anonymous for nearly twenty years.

His first wife came from an abusive background. "She argued and I learned to ignore her. I felt like a failure. After the divorce, I didn't have any money and had a bad car. As I felt I needed things, I'd take them, like driving away without paying for gas. *I felt God had left me so I left God.* Maybe I was impatient."

Robert's second wife came from Russia. As a Roman Catholic, he still struggled with guilt over his divorce and remarriage. On top of this he stated: "Theft is common in Russia but my wife is very honest." He could not bring himself to tell his wife yet about his recent arrest.

Robert primarily overspent on clothes. *"I always felt good when I was wearing something new. I got a high from it. In the beginning, I would buy and buy.* Then there was a time that I returned things I bought. Eventually, I began to just steal them. The last time I shoplifted was yesterday."

Robert had begun taking anti-depressants over the last year or so and then stopped them six weeks ago. "They were $50/month and weren't helping me stop shoplifting," he said.

I asked Robert to call his doctor about his medication. I also asked him to immediately start avoiding stores. He stated he would try but by our next session he relayed the following story: "We had a wedding at our house—for my stepdaughter—and my wife told me to go to the store. I managed to stay focused." We discussed how his wife needed to be involved more with the shopping and refrain from asking him to go to stores—at least for a while.

Robert began avoiding stores but, naturally, he started feeling withdrawal symptoms. "I'm not good with emotions. I've noticed a lot of sensitivity and irritability. But I know I have a choice in my reaction—I don't have to act on my thoughts or temptations. *Wow, I can really see how shopping and shoplifting were highs and rewards for me.*"

Slowly, Robert developed a more disciplined and consistent regimen around his food and diet, work, physical training, and writing. He was filling up his time and enjoying spending it well. He was feeling more grounded, balanced, and good about himself. He also started opening up more in his weekly A.A. men's group meeting.

Robert asked me whether he should invest any money in getting a personal trainer. I suggested that he might do so only if he could find it within his budget. He also realized how he needed to set up more activities with his son that didn't involve shopping/spending. *"I don't want to teach my son that all there is to do is shop and spend money."* He began to feel more proud of himself and his fathering, his wisdom that he was passing onto his son.

As our therapy progressed, Robert got more in touch with his feelings of deep unworthiness and rage. During one session, he shared: "The other day, I did everything around my house and spent time with my kid. My wife came in at end of day and asked: 'what have you been doing all day?' I snapped."

He tried to trace back the roots of his despair. "My mother ruled the family and Dad was very passive. My wife is like my Mom—she has a strong personality. She needs to change her language. I guess I'm like my Dad."

It became increasingly clear that Robert's history of drinking, shopping and spending, and shoplifting were efforts to both muffle his emotions as well as to act them out—as I bluntly suggested—"a big 'Fuck you!'"

Robert agreed to go back on Prozac to help him manage his anger and his continued urges to both shop and shoplift. The next step for him was to get honest with his wife about his arrest. When he finally told her, he felt relieved and, to his surprise, so did she. Apparently, she suspected he was withholding the truth form her about something.

"The only problem is," he shared, "I think she may want a divorce now. I'm sure her two grown daughters will tell her to leave me."

I suggested we schedule an emergency two-hour session with his wife. She agreed to participate but called me prior to our session to give me a head's up on some difficult issues: "He's lied to me about his unpaid taxes before we got married. He owed 5 years worth of taxes, nearly $50,000. We eventually borrowed the money from his brother. I ended up paying most of it back myself. He has leaned on me for 13 years. I'm afraid he'll fall if I leave."

During our joint counseling session, I encouraged Robert's wife to share out loud what she shared with me privately. She did. Robert listened and seemed to have a hard time hearing this. "I'm mad, too!" he raised his voice. You incurred $40,000 in debt going to art school!" Then to me he shared: "she says I have a split personality. Maybe I do. It's like I've become my ex-wife: up and down. *I've not been a strong husband. I'm angry at her and at myself. I have to*

26

stand up for myself. I feel like I'm not able to protect or defend myself. My Dad never stood up to my Mom. I don't want a divorce."

Other long-suppressed issues and feelings were expressed during our joint session. Both partners seemed exhausted by the end of it. Time would tell where things would lead.

A week later, during our next session, Robert was upbeat. He shared that his wife was happy he's in therapy and that she didn't want to hurt their son by getting a divorce. He also shared that she had been affectionate toward him but they were sleeping in separate bedrooms now.

"I started packing up things and letting things go. We're selling our house. We're hoping to buy a smaller one. I'm also exploring anger counseling. We've been talking some more. She told me she went to art school so she could get a job to help pay my debt."

As we focused more on Robert's shopping and spending, a light bulb went on for him: *"Money was my button, my religion."* He then elaborated about how his father didn't buy him many things when he was a child. *"I just wanted love, attention. It didn't have to be new stuff. I didn't buy my daughter a lot of things either—but my first wife did. But with my son now, I seemed to be making up for lost time.*

"It's funny, my wife's former husband berated her for her spending—now I'm the one buying things all the time. Her first husband was very tight with money. I was different. *She thought she saw generosity in me but it was not coming from generosity but from insecurity... Bob isn't good enough without something."*

So, Robert came to this deep and painful awareness or supposed truth: "Bob isn't good enough without something." Is that true? I asked. "I don't know," he said. *"I have this*

27

drive to be the best; I don't know why my image is so important. I have to remember my worth is on the inside."

I gave him an affirmation to practice saying to himself: *"Bob is good enough as he is and he doesn't need things to feel good about himself or for others to like him."*

He then changed the topic. "I'm going camping with my son this weekend and I have this brand new kayak that I bought not long ago. *I notice when I buy something new it's like the newness and purity of nature. I've always had this desire for something new and beautiful.* But my wife wants me to take it back. She actually demanded I do it. It's going to be hard but I'm going to do it. I have to prove to her and to myself that I can do this. I just hope they'll take it back."

During Robert's next session, he told me he had a successful camping trip with his son. He focused on the quality of time spent rather than buying things or spending a lot of money together. He was also pleased that the store he bought his kayak from took it back. But then he got quiet.

"My wife put an offer on a house of her own. I don't think she wants to live with me. It's a body blow. We're in marital counseling together though. I don't know what's going to happen. I'm trying not to make waves with her. I didn't say 'come to America and live like a queen.' I should have told her the truth at the beginning about my problems but her husband had an affair on her and I just didn't want her to mistrust me either. I don't even know why she loves me."

I let Robert vent his thoughts and emotions like waves washing over him. I encouraged him to seek out a divorce support group—just in case. I also recommended that he stay out of stores and double-up on his A.A. meetings.

At our next session, Robert shared how he was just feeling very betrayed by life. The full brunt of his foolishness with money also weighed upon him. He shared how he and his wife quickly sold their house and that they were now preparing to move; the only question was whether they would be moving together. "I asked her why she loved me—what she saw in me. She said 'gentleness and kindness.'"

He sought out an attorney—just in case the divorce moved forward. He shared how he left his first wife everything without a fight. He knew he had to find a happy medium this time without getting too adversarial.

"I'll survive if she leaves me. I will be very lonely but I won't relapse—not on alcohol, not on shoplifting, not on shopping. I can cook and clean and take care of myself. *I'm learning to care more about how I manage money. I'm working on saying no to things my son wants but I'm also telling him it's not his fault that I'm not buying as many things for him.* I know I need to work on my anger. I don't know why I haven't cried yet. The last time I cried was when my mother died when I was 9 years old."

Again, it became clear to me that this man was a well-spring of unexpressed grief. His shopping and spending and drinking and shoplifting were all attempts to both feel something and to not feel something. Men, especially, feel anger as their primary emotion while hiding many others. But Robert had repressed even his anger. I shared these thoughts with him and we continued to explore this.

The next week, Robert left me a phone message to say that he was feeling less tense and was letting go of his marriage. "I was traveling for business and treated myself to the oxygen and massage spa at the airport. There are some good things happening. I'll see you next week," he added.

A few days later Robert called me to cancel his next appointment. "My wife and I are getting back together." I heard from Robert recently by e-mail. He was doing well.

Notes & Reflections:

<u>Lynne's Story</u>—The Bargain/Image/Co-Dependent Shopper

Lynne is a woman in her mid-thirties who describes herself as a life-long "bargain shopper." Her behavior got out of hand recently after the births of her two young children. She overspent, hid her purchases from her husband, and even had a brief foray into price tag switching—a form of shoplifting.

I am what I call "a bargain shopper." I've been into clothes since age 6. I'm married and have two young girls. Things got worse after the births of my children. I had post-partum depression after my second girl was born and probably had it after my first. I've been on anti-depressants for several years. *I have this innate need to please others. I try to do things to get affirmation. I think I learned this from my mother.*

Also around the time of my first child's birth, my Dad died. This was 2001. He had handled all of our family's money. After his death, we found out he had spend pretty much everything and left my Mom with almost nothing. She was more of the saver/penny pincher compared to my Dad. Of course, it became even worse after his death.

I guess I'm more like my Dad in the spending department. I also have had problems with overeating, over-exercising and, more recently, with shoplifting. I started switching price tags a few years ago. I don't know if that's stealing. But I finally told my husband recently about this and he is supportive of my stopping this and getting my shopping and spending under control.

I don't really know myself. I've always put other people first. Everyone thinks I'm just this little innocent, sweet down-to-earth person but I'm not. I have my moods. I have a poor self-image. My husband is such a good person in every way. He's my moral compass. He can't understand why I do what I do. He's tried to help me in many ways. I want to be better for him and my kids. I don't think June Cleaver would ever switch a price tag. I know I can be so much more.

My husband has tried to help me in different ways but he can't. I've been to a couple of local counselors but I don't think they understand my over-shopping and I was embarrassed to bring up the price tag switching. *I feel like I'm living this lie and pretending to be something I'm not.* I don't want to do anything unethical and wind up in prison. I want to be a good role model for my kids.

I want to be happy and I don't even know what that means. I want it to come from within—not from buying or giving all this stuff. But I'm such a martyr. If I cook a meatloaf and burn it, I'd always take the burnt piece. My mother was the same way. Like I said, I'm a bargain shopper. I'm Jewish—maybe it's cultural. I don't know. When we go to the restaurant, I'll almost always order the cheapest thing on the menu but I don't expect that of others. I think about trying different things but I feel guilty when I give myself anything.

I have so many things at home that I don't even use—from food to clothing to toiletries—all kinds of odds and ends. I went to Wal-Mart the other day and didn't over-shop or change any price tags. I felt great! So, I know that's the direction I need to move in. When I over-shop or switch tags, I get a little rush or something but I end up feeling all tense and conflicted. But the temptations are still there. I took my daughter to TJ Maxx to get an outfit and couldn't find anything for her and then I just started to browse around for something for myself. The deals were insane! But I left without buying anything.

Another thing I have to be careful about is the U-Scan self-serve check-outs at stores. I have slipped some things by that one without paying, too. I feel disgusted with myself. Then I overeat and it all becomes this vicious cycle of disgust. I really need help.

It's funny, though, in my work life I am a pretty centered, organized, and competent person. I have a psychology degree so I ought to know how to help myself but I guess I can't. I started attending Alanon, too, and that's helping.

I went shopping with my husband the other day for a few things for Halloween. Good thing he was there or I would have bought the store. The last thing I need—or my kids need—is a lot of extra candy sitting around. *I have to slow down and remember that the holidays aren't about buying but about family.*

I think part of what I'm going through is grief over the loss of my Dad—there's definitely a void there. I also don't want to sound like I'm blaming my husband but he isn't the most romantic guy anymore. He tells me I'm pretty on occasion but not often. Like most men, I guess, he watches a lot of TV. He needs to do more but I'm reluctant to speak up— especially after the problems I've caused with my shopping and spending. But it becomes like a cat chasing its tail.

We hardly go out anymore. Part of it is because we're trying to watch what we spend and part of it is my mother wants to come out with us and I don't like spending time with her. She's selfish. She wants sympathy and affirmation but doesn't give it to others. Her whole world revolves around money. She's the one who taught me how to bargain shop and even to shoplift—a long time ago.

I did have lunch with her last week and told her about my therapy. At first, she had this tone like I'm doing something wrong. Then she said "I hope your husband doesn't blame me for what went wrong." I told her it's not about her, it's about me. *My mother and I, all we ever did together was shop. When I was in college, we'd get together every Saturday and shop. After college, we'd still go shopping and if there wasn't a price tag on something, she'd find a tag to put on it.* I talked to her about this a while ago and she denied this. But I know what I saw. We have a long way to go in getting honest and real.

I looked up to my Mom. I wish she had stood up for herself more with my Dad. Even now, *she loves to play the victim; I don't like victims yet I have this tendency, too.*

At my Alanon meeting recently there were about ten people—all women—and most had been coming to the meeting for a long time and had been married to alcoholics or came from alcoholic families. I couldn't relate to that. My husband is pretty stable and my father was responsible. I had a good relationship with him. He was home every day for dinner with us by 6. It's the opposite with my husband. If anything, he's a bit of a workaholic. Even after our kids were born, he never even took any extra time off work. The only thing that was similar was my Dad watched a lot of TV, too.

I think part of the key to my change is to allow myself an occasional reward. I don't know if I rewarded myself this past week but this Saturday I will go out to a restaurant and order what I want. *I'm also learning to pay for things more with cash. My husband is helping with the shopping and, truthfully, I think it's better if I just stay out of stores for a long time.* I don't fear so much falling back. I just want my husband to know how much I do around the house, with the kids, and working. I'd like him to help out more, appreciate all I do, and take some ownership with things.

I am going through withdrawal from shopping. I feel a bit depressed and am having trouble exercising. I can also feel this intense anger coming up toward my Mom. I also am on edge with my husband. I did a good job, though, the other night when we went out to eat. We went to a Japanese restaurant and I ordered what I wanted to eat. I even ordered a beer. I never order a beer out. It felt a little awkward but I think it was a big step.

There is one thing that I do remember being mad at my Dad about. When my husband and I were dating back in our late teens, my Dad didn't like him and basically shut me out for a while because I wouldn't break up with him. Even my Mom didn't speak to me for a few months. And then my husband—who was my boyfriend at the time—ended up cheating on me. I felt lost and alone. I moved to another state for a while and, eventually, reconnected with my husband-to-be and my parents. When my Dad died in 2001 I was so in denial about his illness and impending death.

I'm continuing to see the connection between my overgiving and my over-shopping and even shoplifting. I also see the connection between my husband not being fully present and my getting angry and feeling hurt and rejected. It's like he embodies the detached and selfish aspects of my Mom and Dad and I get triggered. I'm becoming more assertive, though. I've asked him to pick my up some flowers and he has done this a few times.

The other day my back was hurting and I asked if I could just talk to him for a few minutes and my back felt better afterwards. He doesn't get it, though. I ask him for help with other things and he doesn't always do it right away but he's pretty good about it. I just worry that he may not like the person I'm becoming. I feel so different. We need major improvements in our level of intimacy. It's me, too. I want him to talk to me more and tell me how he feels. I don't feel special. There's still this big wall between us.

The good news is that since I've stopped going to the stores I have been starting to eat less and eat healthier and burn off some of my stress by exercising. My husband and I are going to sit down and make a list of all the things I do and we're going to split them up—a new division of labor. We also are doing a budget together. I wanted to buy a dress for a big date but I talked myself out of it. We already had a big credit card bill. I think my husband appreciated my ability to set limits. He trusts me more. Unfortunately, there are still times I don't trust him. I'll never forget when he cheated on me. I wish I would have been strong enough to say "fuck you" to him and to my parents—they let me down, too. I need to tell him this. *I think maybe my shopping is related to my resentments as well.*

Note: After 10 sessions of therapy with me—including the fifth and last session with her husband—Lynne's medication dosages were lowered and she reported feeling much happier, more centered, and more capable of making clear, good decisions. She and her husband were getting along better and their level of intimacy improved greatly. She also reported that she had some heart-to-heart talks with her mother which went well. She was ecstatic that her mother had become more interested in seeing her grandchildren and helping out with them more frequently.

Lynne was aware she also needed to spend some time and energy grieving the death of her father in 2001. She had been so out of control that she did what most people do: put grief on a backburner and try to just move on with life. At my urging, she committed to seek out and attend a grief and loss support group. She also was looking to continue therapy with a local counselor.

Lynne's husband continued to do most of the shopping. She reported a relapse or two of going shopping for groceries when her husband was unavailable and she became impatient. "I felt euphoric," she said. This reminded her how shopping remains like a drug for her. "It was a wake-up call again."

Notes & Reflections:

<u>Lucy's Story</u>—The Compulsive/Bargain/Image Shopper

Lucy, 42, has had spending problems her entire life. A survivor of traumatic sexual abuse and assault, she lost her only son in an accident several years ago. Her marriage is at a breaking point and she describes herself as "splitting apart." She sought out specialized help after a brief hospitalization and then taking time off work.

I've been spending most of my life. I come from a large family and feel like I was deprived. I married pretty young and divorced about twenty years ago. I had one child from that marriage. My ex-husband abused me in all ways—verbally, emotionally, physically, and sexually. I'd also been sexually abused—raped—by both friends and strangers. *I've had a lot of traumatic experiences and feel like I have no real choices in life.* I've tried counseling, read several books on over-shopping, and gone to Debtors Anonymous meetings. For whatever reason, they've been of limited value.

I started compulsively scrap-booking and then started buying clothes. I just spent $1,000 the other day. I've been remarried almost 10 years and my husband found these clothes—*I was hoarding and hiding them.* He's really on top of what I do. He's ready to divorce me over the debt. I had one card with a $23,000 credit limit that I maxed out. I just got another card with a $15,000 limit. I also impulsively bought a brand new car and new furniture. I'm in debt at least $100,000.

I've been taking anti-depressants since my son died three years ago in a car accident. He was just 18. I'm also on anti-anxiety meds and sleeping pills. I've gained over 40 pounds in the last few years. I can stop eating for a while but then I binge and sometimes purge, throw up. I've had major cosmetic surgery over the last few years. I've also had fibromyalgia for many years. It's been flaring up bad lately.

I feel out of control all around. I know I'm trying to numb the pain or fill this void. I just can't stop it. I tried to commit suicide nearly 15 years ago and still think about it but wouldn't do it. I'm afraid of going to Hell. I'm a Christian.

When I shop, I feel euphoric. I have to get a good deal, though. I'm not saying I'm cheap and just buy inexpensive things. I'm trying to only shop with my husband now. *I just want to figure out what's driving me. I know my son's death is part of it but I've had this problem long before that.*

I feel like I've never had any friends, real friends. I feel like I was deprived economically. My folks were religious and our religion seemed to say "store food." I had a dishonest or sneaky streak growing up. I took food when I could. Then I was sexually assaulted—gang raped—when I was 18. I had some family members who were inappropriate with me, too. I even got raped by people in the military.

I got married young and my husband abused me so I left him when my son was almost 2. I didn't want him growing up in an abusive home. That was the smartest thing I've ever done. *But I was angry at life, angry at God. I felt so betrayed.* I got back into the party scene. Then I got raped again by this guy I was dating and my life started to unravel even further. *He tied me up with my own clothes and raped me.*

You'd think I would have gotten into alcohol or drugs—I tried them—but they never did it for me. Shopping did. I had all these clothes that I'd bought and somehow clothes make me feel pretty, make me fit in, feel secure. I'm the kind of shopper who doesn't even try things on and then gets home and feel ugly. It's ironic this guy used my own clothes to tie me up and rape me.

I also feel like I gave up on my dream career. I was going to be a marine biologist. I wanted to work with the whales and the dolphins and the endangered species. Everyone discouraged me. I was stupid enough to listen to them.

So, I started this other profession—working with criminal offenders. My current husband was in this field and got me a job. Then, shortly after starting work, my ex-husband filed papers to get custody of our son. Because of my fragile state, he was able to do it. My son was about 10 at the time.

I was devastated. I actually had a nervous breakdown and was off work. I was already in debt from college loans and was on welfare. I wasn't shopping so much then—even when I was depressed. *It seemed like when I shopped it was to attract a man.* My current husband isn't as much into clothes or how I look though. I like to be alone when I shop—it makes me feel better.

It's as if I've compartmentalized my life into three distinct faces or personalities. One face—with my husband—I act fine, at least in front of him. A second face—when alone—I just fall apart. A third face—at work—I'm barely holding it together. It's hard.

I feel guilt-ridden over my son's death even though I can't cry anymore and just act like I don't have a son. I was supposed to be with him the day he died. He wasn't wearing a seatbelt. *Maybe I'm punishing myself.* That's what a few people have told me.

Lately, when I do go shopping, I try to go with somebody. All my friends know I've got a problem. They won't let me overspend when I'm with them. It kind of upsets me at times. I asked my husband recently to buy me a shirt and he said "no." I was mad but I settled down. I have started to shop more online. I have a computer in the closet and I bought some stuff secretly. I had a coupon that said: "if you buy an item you get 20% off and if you buy a third item you get 40% off." *It's ridiculous. I didn't even feel that good afterward. They're all expendable items and short-lived. I threw all my magazines out and then went back and pulled a few out of the trash. It's like I was a drug addict.*

I'm so in debt I have to get out. I feel good when I pay a bill off but then I want to reward myself by buying something. Is that insane or what? I have these shopping blackouts. Honestly, I really don't remember spending money on half of what I buy. I've tried to give myself an allowance. My husband suggested I spend $150 a month on clothes. I tried it but couldn't do it. I'd always go way over. I know some shopaholics buy and return. But I don't like returning things. It's a headache.

I've taken off work for a few weeks—sick leave—so I can minimize my stress and focus on this counseling program. The good news is I live in a town with no Mall. I have to stay put and off the computer now. I did buy a few books on Amazon. I've resisted shopping—not because I'm not tempted—because I'm trying to save my marriage. My eating isn't good now but I'm just watching a lot of movies at home. I'm trying to cancel as many catalogues as possible.

I also feel like this is time to try to reconnect with my husband. He has a lot of resentment toward me. I have a lot toward him, too. He's not been that attentive to me over the last few years—even since my son died. I think it affected him, too. All I'd like is some kind words and some touch but he refuses. He says I should know that he loves me. He doesn't abuse me but now I feel like I'm neglected. Of course, when I neglect him, there's hell to pay. So I do my best to give him attention.

There are periods when I don't shop and I feel like my husband doesn't even give me any credit. I starve myself from spending. I never know what kind of mood he's in. 9 out of 10 times he says "it's not about you." We're down to just two Visa cards. *We try to consult with each other about any purchases and that's been working a little better.*

We recently prepared for a trip and I wanted to buy a gown. My husband said okay if it was reasonably priced. I bought it and a couple of other small things. I showed him the items and the receipts. He seemed okay with it. I felt good about not overspending. *It's like a double-edged sword though. On the one hand, I resent the fact that I have to report to him and earn his trust. On the other hand, I actually think he's too trusting of me at this point. It's confusing.*

Right now I'm still trying to moderate my shopping. If I were to go cold turkey it would be feast or famine—I don't know if I could go very long without spending anything. I did well on the gown—I paid $100—but then I bought some other stuff that I didn't tell my husband about—for about $200. I was with this friend who is not good for me to hang around. She's a shopaholic, too. I recently had to tell her I can't go to the Mall with her anymore. She was a bit upset, I could tell, but that's how it's gonna be.

I finally made an appointment to go to a grief and loss support group. There's also a book I found about compulsive shopping from a Christian perspective. *At times, I can feel this subtle peace when I'm not shopping. But I also feel the agitation and restlessness, too.*

Christmas is coming up fast and I know that's going to be a tough time for me. My husband says he'll help me. There are some expensive gifts I'd like to buy for him and for me and there's some expensive gifts I'd love to receive from him. I guess I'm going to have to go more low-key this year. *As for the rest of my family, they all see my shopping addiction as a joke. Fortunately, I'm not close to them. I'm not expecting much from them and they're not expecting much from me.*

The other thing I've started to work on is getting rid of the clutter in my house—most of it is stuff I bought and don't need anymore. It feels good to let go of all this junk from the past. It's just been weighing me down.

I had a good trip with my husband recently and didn't spend much. We bought a few things for others and I bought myself some bath salts for $6. *I had this realization on the trip: the reason I over-shop is I don't feel like I'm worth much. I'm always trying to look better and be accepted.* When I go out, I compete with other women. I look at other women and see how good some of them look. *My husband never says to me "You look so good."*

In my mind, I know I'm worth something intellectually—I busted my ass for my college degree. But I was told many times in my life that I was just a "dumb blonde." I'm in my 40's now and I'm getting old. *My husband looks at younger women but he won't look at me. How can I compete? I dress like a teen. Maybe I'm trying to hold onto my youth.*

Sometimes my husband threatens to divorce me—if not because of the shopping than because of my weight. I'd probably be lonelier if he did leave me—and I'd probably continue shopping and spending. That's the sad part. He's a workaholic so he'd be okay if he was single. *The truth is: he's incapable of love. I've been hoping for him to change but he won't—even if I stopped shopping and lost 50 pounds.*

I need more compassionate people in my life. I need more people who see me as me—who see the good, the strengths, people who uplift me. I'm having some success in curtailing my shopping and, even more so, my spending. I did buy a few little items but they were on sale. I'm starting to feel more optimistic. I even returned some things to the store that I had bought a while ago—and I don't like returning things.

I went to my son's grave site the other day. It's the first time in a long time that I've gone there. I was mad that nobody is taking care of the site. I felt a little numb but I'm glad I went. I think I'll visit more regularly.

My Dad retired last week and me and my Mom went out for lunch. I told my Mom what's going on with me. I can be honest with her about my life. I grew up as a loving person, sensitive, I could feel what others feel.

I've stayed out of the stores even with all the advertisements. Part of me is glad I did and the other part wonders what I missed. My husband asks me about the coupons. He's not been too helpful lately. He wanted me to go down to the stores. He got tired of shopping. We got into a big blow-up. He didn't get me anything for Christmas and I asked him why not? He said I always go to get my own gifts. He told me I didn't need anything. I told him it's not about what I needed, about what I wanted. He told me I'd get over it. He told me I'm in debt and betrayed him. I told him he acts like we're just roommates not lovers. He told me I'm the most selfish person because when I buy it's for me and when he spends it's for us. He said he's sick of it. I asked him: you're telling me that I have to get out of debt first before I get any affection? He told me if I'm looking for the lovey-dovey guy he's not it and to look elsewhere. I told him he was at the beginning but he downplayed that.

More recently, my husband has been taking some steps to not ignore me. We were watching a video on his laptop and he told me he loves me and wants to work on our relationship. I told him: I'm doing the best I can. He said, "I know." *It may take a long time before I'm really well. I don't even want to go shopping anymore. The thought of it makes me sick to my stomach now.*

I started the grief group and I already met a woman whose son died in a car accident at 35. It feels good to connect. I'm going back to work soon, though. That will be an adjustment. I can see why they say "one day at a time."

Notes and Reflections

<u>Jeremy's Story</u>—The Compulsive/Image Shopper

Jeremy, 20, found out about my counseling services after several prosecutions for shoplifting and employee theft. It became clear early in our work together that he had multiple and complex issues including over-shopping and overspending, and alcohol and drug dependence—mostly prescription painkillers. He was facing a long jail sentence.

Jeremy was adopted by his current family when he was just 6 weeks old. His adoptive family also had foster kids in their home which Jeremy described as disruptive. As an "only child," he stated *"I didn't want to share my parents with the other kids in the house."* He eventually found out some information about his biological parents—stating they were diagnosed as "schizophrenic." By the time he came to work with me, he had been in counseling for nearly 15 years, had been on and off many different medications, and had been diagnosed as bi-polar and chemically dependent.

Jeremy acknowledged he tends to make "poor choices" and reported remorse over many of his actions. He related several criminal offenses: felony embezzlement (from a retail store) at age 16; misdemeanor shoplifting from a Mall at age 19 (for which he remained on probation); misdemeanor minor in possession of alcohol at age 19; and a more recent misdemeanor shoplifting charge which triggered a violation of his current probation.

Jeremy seemed to feel that most of his behavioral problems began about 4 years ago when he was kicked out of his Catholic high school at the beginning of his junior year for bringing a BB gun to school. He got into drugs and alcohol around this time. He found himself in a public high school in a tough urban city. He began stealing in various forms, perhaps in reaction to the stress of his situation. He reported that he even stole money and items from his family and expressed remorse about this.

Jeremy used shopping and stealing to soothe himself and to win over friends by giving them or selling them goods he bought or stole. Jeremy appeared to have a strong desire to be popular and to be the center of attention. Jeremy himself recognized a profound preoccupation with his looks and image, especially his clothing and fashion. He also had a passion and some real talent for writing poetry and songs—hip-hop and rap.

Jeremy had a total lack of confidence in his ability to save and manage his money—whether it was an allowance or a small paycheck. He also seemed to both crave and fear being alone. By the time he began seeing me, he had become involved in a local church and was making some new friends there. *He recognized that a key to successfully changing his life would be avoiding friends who drank, used drugs, stole, or seemed to be more materialistic and superficial.* He also wanted to pursue his other interests: soccer, psychology, and writing poems and songs.

Jeremy had major unresolved conflicts about his identity, his life's path, and coming to terms with his past actions. I suggested he could benefit from some good mentoring—maybe through Big Brothers or someone at his church. I also encouraged him to channel his emotions into his writing and music and reminded him that many past and current writers and musicians used their lives as a well for expression and that many had found a voice in "recovery" from which to speak. Jeremy was a fan of the rock band Aerosmith which was a shining example of this.

Jeremy also seemed to struggle with narcissism and grandiosity—the shadow or flip sides of intense shame and feelings of inadequacy and inferiority. Helping him find a

47

path of a more slow and steady pace would be challenging but essential.

Jeremy continued on several medications, came to see me for counseling—unfortunately, only every 2-3 weeks—and was ordered to stay off drugs and alcohol (he was being randomly drug tested by the courts). He also attended C.A.S.A. (Cleptomaniacs And Shoplifters Anonymous) meetings weekly to every 2 weeks. I advised him to find work and/or enroll in community college classes toward getting a psychology degree. I admonished him against going to stores where he might shop, spend, or steal.

For a while, Jeremy seemed to be making progress—he seemed to be re-building his self-esteem from the inside-out rather than the outside-in. He slowly took a quasi-leadership role at C.A.S.A. and bonded with that group and his recovery group at his church. Unfortunately, he suffered emotionally when his grandmother died just shy of his 21st birthday. He was very close to her. He also acknowledged temptations to go to the bar with some old friends on his 21st birthday. He ended up following through with this and then fell off his semi-regular attendance at C.A.S.A. and with counseling.

If ever there was a case of someone struggling for a clear sense of identity, it was Jeremy. I haven't heard anything from him or about him in over two years. I wish him well.

Notes & Reflections:

Helena's Story—The Compulsive/Image Shopper

Helena is a 51 year-old Hispanic-American, married, with a full-time job and a quick wit and good sense of humor. She had episodes of over-shopping in her early adult life but it subsided until more recently when a series of losses appeared to disrupt her equilibrium. She sought help to save her marriage and regain her sense of self.

I saw Mr. Shulman on The Montel Williams Show on July 3, 2006. The show was on shopping addiction. It couldn't have aired at a better time. I called him immediately and enrolled in his phone counseling program.

I've been married about 8 years and have been over-shopping for about that long, maybe a bit longer. It was threatening my marriage. I've been overspending around $1,000 per month. Maybe that doesn't sound like much—but it adds up quickly. I also worked with a local group that addresses credit and spending issues. My Mom passed away about 8 years ago, too. And then my father passed away just last year.

I sought help because my husband found out recently about my problem. I'd been keeping it from him. I was writing checks that kept overdrawing my account and he finally discovered this. I guess it was a blessing. Fortunately, he sees I have a problem and wants me to get help.

Where to begin? I'm bipolar and have been on medication the last 6 years. Even though my shopping and spending has gotten out of control mostly in the last 8-10 years, I had some issues with it many years ago. I remember when I was about 23 and just graduated from college, I had my first real job and was working in New York City. I wasn't making much and was living with my parents. I started making and saving more money. I was living in mid-town. *When I got my first pay check I went out shopping—for clothes! I felt excited. It was like a reward to myself. But I also felt guilty for some reason, too.*

I had a new outfit for every day. The other women at work seemed to wear the same outfits. They called me "the clotheshorse." It made me feel good. I went from being a plain Jane to a trendy star. I got more confidence. I didn't have a lot of confidence growing up.

I know something snapped after my Mom died just before my first marriage. We were very close. I also had lingering grief over my first husband's death from cancer 12 years ago. We were married 4 years. We were going to have kids together but we put it on hold when he got sick. I found out during his illness and after his death that he had been spent a lot of money and hid it from me. His mother took away this box of all these papers and bills. *I ended up being held responsible for his debts. I had to declare bankruptcy prior to getting married to my current husband. So, that was another thing I went through. But I started to overspend right away.*

My first husband duped me. He wasn't working when I first met him. Then he got into managing a business that he told me he was going to own and then sell for a million dollars. I believed him. That's what you get for meeting somebody through a personal ad. But I can only blame myself. I was in such a hurry to get married. My parents didn't approve of anyone I was dating.

I'm Hispanic and we were very poor growing up. My family was very frugal. I didn't have many clothes when I was young. We were brought up strict Catholic and there were a lot of rules. I always did my best to obey. I went to church every Sunday. My first husband wasn't very religious. He was very controlling though. He wouldn't let me see my sister—he said she was wild. I regretted going along with this because I didn't have a relationship with her again until after he died. I must have been afraid of him.

Anyway, after getting my first real job and after getting married, I'd go on these occasional shopping sprees. I'd buy clothing, jewelry, books—it made me feel like I had this power. It's funny, though, because most of the stuff I bought ended up in the closet, barely used. I felt independent for the first time in my life. I was only spending about 10% of my income. *Then I got credit cards. In almost no time, I ran up $6,000 in debt—and that was almost 20 years ago.* I had to clamp down. I ended up taking most of the things back or donating them to charity. It was mostly stuff for me. I rarely bought things for others.

I guess I fell back into the same pattern over the last 8-10 years. I thought I'd learned my lesson the first time. It's been frustrating. *I've heard a lot of bipolar people over-shop or overspend. I'm on meds and they don't even seem to work.*

Early in my counseling with Mr. Shulman, I remember I went to Disney World with my husband and I was trying not to shop. I was surprised at my urges. I usually bought anything and everything—tee shirts, stuffed animals. I had to leave the park for a bit to regain my composure. My husband was surprised, too. *It hurts to say no to myself. It's like I've lost something. I feel like a baby. But I felt better afterwards.*

Mr. Shulman asked me if I had any other family members who were shopaholics. I remembered my Mom would buy five loaves of bread and different kinds of cookies. She loaded up, hoarded things. I wondered why she did that. *Then I remembered: she lived through The Great Depression and didn't have much food as a kid. Food is one thing, but I had 300 pairs of shoes! I admit I want to look better than the next woman but I don't really need to impress anybody.*

I've wondered if any of my shopping had to do with a nervous breakdown I had 20 years ago. I was suicidal and hospitalized on and off for 13 years. I had been transferred at my job and hated it and then my boyfriend at the time left me. Looking back on it, I can't understand why these events affected me that much but they did. *Maybe my self-esteem was damaged and I tried to get it back by buying nice things.*

The reality is I have a hole to dig out of now—both financially and emotionally. Neither my husband nor I are working right now and I don't want to file for bankruptcy again. All I can pay right now is the minimum balances.

In our therapy session with my husband, he admitted he was in denial about my shopping and spending and just turned a blind eye. He has seen me become more confident since everything's out in the open. I've seemed to have fewer mood swings, too. He had to stand up to me and not be afraid of my temper tantrums. He's done a pretty good job so far. I think he's afraid of acting like a policeman or a parent.

A big part of my saving my marriage was taking full responsibility for my behavior and sincerely apologizing for it. I'm still trying to understand more clearly why I did what I did but, in the meantime, I need to stick to my promises and that's how you rebuild trust. My husband is very concerned about lies and dishonesty. He asked me if there was anything else I bought that he should know about and I said "no." Then, a few days later, a package arrived in the mail with some items that I don't even remember ordering. He didn't believe me at first. But I told him, I swear, I must have blacked out—that's how bad it got. We weren't getting our bank statements on time for some reason and he thought I was intercepting them. Then an old credit card bill came through and he hit the roof. I can understand his paranoia.

The sad reality is that we both are in our 50's now and we hope to retire eventually but we hardly have any savings or retirement funds. That's scary. But I'm learning to be careful about thinking too far ahead. It's good to get a reality check but I don't want to become hopeless either.

All in all, I feel a lot happier since I haven't over-shopped. I actually like myself again. I feel like I'm back to my real self. I am getting back this sense of power. My problem is going to be Christmas. But I don't have any credit or debit cards to use. I'm going to plan ahead and allot a small amount to spend and take my husband with me. *In the meantime, I try to treat myself to small purchases—like a book: that'll keep my occupied for a week or so.*

I've also realized that I want to be heard. I want my freedom, too. I was restricted a lot in life—by my parents and by my first husband.

I called Debtors Anonymous but it didn't seem like a good fit. I wish there was a group called Shopaholics Anonymous.

I've had 50 days clean so far. I'm back to work. I want to start a support group. I'm speaking up more I don't feel powerless or weak anymore. I've never felt proud of myself

But I still have to be careful. I had a near miss recently where I got a catalogue in the mail and it said I was "pre-approved for a credit card." *My hands shook and I had to ask my husband to throw it away.*

I also know I still have a lot of healing to do around my parents' deaths. They were good people and it's hard for me to think negative thoughts about them but I do have some resentments. *I was the first person in my family to get a masters degree and my father kind of ignored us and he never said he was proud of me. My Mom was so religious that she told me I was supposed to be a virgin when I married and she knew I wasn't and I felt her disapproval.*

My husband and I continue to make progress in rebuilding our marriage. If anything, I feel like I need to support him more right now. Now that I'm getting myself together he needs some help, too. He really wants to get another job and I know that's stressful for him. Extreme stress is a warning sign for me and I'm not sure how it's going to affect him.

I know he trusts me a lot more, though. He trusts me to get the mail now. He doesn't worry I'm going to hide something from him and that feels good. Eventually, I hope to have access to our checkbook again but I'm not in a hurry. As far as credit cards go, we'll have to wait and see. At this point, I almost don't want to have one ever again. We were at the ATM the other day and I didn't have this feeling of dread that he'd check the balance and find out something was off.

We also got through Christmas with flying colors. We both spent about $100. *I didn't even buy any clothes. I feel like I'm done with that. I'm happy with myself. Putting on a skirt is okay but it's not what makes me who I am. I'm happy with myself—the real me has been hidden.* The last time I was happy was on our wedding day. I can't deal with unhappiness anymore.

While I haven't had any big shopping urges in a while, I'm still a little scared. I'm thinking I'm going to take a year not to shop alone. *I still don't trust myself.* I continue to do self-talk, and to ask my husband for help. I still feel a flutter in my stomach if I look at a catalogue. I have to remember what's important is time with my husband.

Looking back on it all, I think my shopping had to do with being lonely, trying to impress people, being bored and being stressed. I never felt loved or accepted for who I was. I felt unworthy. Shopping covered up those feelings for a while but only made things worse in the long run. I hope I can stay on this new path.

Notes & Reflections:

Rose's Story—The Compulsive/Image Shopper

Rose, 60, is a creative, artsy, spiritual "free-spirit" who was brought up in a wealthy family with financial dysfunctions. A successful entrepreneur, she lives in one of the most expensive parts of the country. After a recent divorce and illness, she fell into deep debt—pulled herself out with the help of her father—and fell back into debt again soon after. She is coming to terms with aging, a declining income, and taking responsibility for her own financial health.

When Rose called me, she was in about $150,000 of debt. A self-employed entrepreneur nearing 60, she didn't know how many working years she had left in her. She had several college degrees and little savings and no retirement plan. She lived in one of the most high-end areas of the country.

Rose ran up this debt in a matter of a few years after having gotten out of debt when her father bailed her out. *"Shopping is like a sport to me,"* she said dryly.

She had a short marriage that ended in divorce and it was clear she was still recovering from that. "He swept me off my feet. We had this really expensive wedding." She wondered if he left her in part because of her spending habits and debt. She confessed to being incredibly lonely and understood that her shopping was a salve for that. Her spending took many forms: clothes, jewelry, trips, dining out, spiritual classes, and other odds and ends.

The biggest problem, I told her, was that her income was far lower than even her living expenses. She agreed with my assessment but still seemed to be in a state of denial. She lived in an expensive home in an expensive town and had home equity loans and property taxes to pay. Even with her father's bail-out and his annual generous gift of cash to her, the reality was that she couldn't make it on her own. While her ex-husband didn't contribute that much money, when he left there was still a gap. She also stated her husband had become violent. They were in therapy prior to their separation but, apparently, it didn't help much.

Rose lived among some of our wealthiest citizens. Everywhere she looked—the high lifestyle was in her face. In her work—which brought her into the homes of the rich and famous—she was constantly reminded of how little she had by comparison. *"I need to dress well and have good jewelry in my line of work, given my clients."* Fair enough, but there are limits, I suggested.

Rose further stated: *"I grew up pretty wealthy and it's a given I need to have this lifestyle. My father always seemed to imply that he'd be there to take care of me but then again, he gives with strings attached.* When he helped me out of debt a few years ago, it was clear he was disappointed with me and that I shouldn't have to ask him for that kind of help again. *I'm afraid to tell him I've fallen so behind again so quickly.* I'm scared of powerful men like my father. Yet, I am drawn to powerful men and I take care of them. I'm a people pleaser. My Mom has nothing to do with finances and she's totally subservient."

Rose shared that she had also spent a lot of money on her husband when they were married—mostly on clothing. She shared how she had two siblings who didn't seem to have the same money or debt issues, even though they grew up with the same father. Her shame was palpable despite her protests.

"I don't feel less than them but I just didn't plan for retirement like they did. They all travel and have two homes. I chose to live a different lifestyle, a more flexible, free-spirited life. During the '80's, business was booming but I didn't save. I spent it all. My husband was a contractor and we put all our money into remodeling my house. It's paid off but my property taxes, equity loan payments, and credit card bills are killing me. I just don't have enough income to stay afloat. And I can't get any more loans. I'd hate to have to sell my home."

I asked Rose what else she spent her money on. There was a boat trip, travel, dining out, an entire wardrobe, and she started another business that had various start-up costs.

Rose found a local Debtors Anonymous meeting—geared especially for business people and entrepreneurs. Her initial reaction was one of excitement and relief. They even gave her some books and literature for free. I strongly encouraged her to continue regular weekly attendance.

We zeroed in on her relationship with her father as an area which, I strongly felt, needed some kind of breakthrough and which was related to her pattern of over-shopping and overspending.

"My father bought my house and put it in joint-tenancy with me to help me out. But he was planning his estate and put the house in a living trust. Somehow, my taxes went up four-fold. I went to him and told him I didn't think this was fair. He's like that: he'll seem like he's helping you but he's really undermining you. Then he gives me this lump sum every year which, of course, is helpful. *My Dad would always say to me that I never had to worry about money, savings, and I believed him. So, why would I ever take care of myself? Yet, he would also tell me to be independent. I got mixed messages. So, I never learned to manage money.*

"I took out this home equity line a few years ago and paid off all my credit card debt. But I got back into debt. During my divorce, I hardly worked, so that set me back. I spent money on therapy and other healing work that didn't really yield much. So, I've tried to take care of myself. I thought I had gotten myself together. I knew I needed to focus on myself. *But I'd take one step forward and then I would do some crazy behavior out of alignment with my value system."*

I asked Rose what her fear was about coming clean with her father that she had gotten into trouble again. She said she was afraid, first, that he'd yell at her and, second, that he'd cut her off from any future help or try to take the house away. I asked her how realistic she thought it was that he'd do that. She couldn't answer. We had some work to do to get her courage up.

I pressed on. In a worst case scenario, if he did cut you off or if you had to sell your house or leave your house, what would happen? She pondered my question for a minute and then said: "well, I wouldn't want that to happen but I guess I'd find a way to survive. I'd either have to sell my stuff or put it in storage and I'd either have to find a small apartment or move somewhere else. I have thought about moving either to a small town or an island somewhere."

Okay, I said. Just know: even in a worst case scenario, you know you'll survive.

"It would be just so much easier if I could meet a man with some money and he could help me out," she exclaimed.

That might be, I said. But the chances of that happening are slim—unless you attract a man with a lot of money who is not so healthy and who is going to extract an unbearable price from you in return. I'm concerned, as well, that you are bitten by the wishful thinking bug, that you're living in a fantasy that somebody's going to rescue you because your Dad has done that—to some degree—and you've done that with others, too. If you can find a way to get out of this one on your own—but with appropriate support—how would that make you feel?

"Pretty good, I guess."

Well, it's possible. There's a path toward financial and emotional health and empowerment—and they're linked.

But Rose's resistance came up. She soon began seeing a man who she'd met at her ballroom dance class. I had asked her to consider staying out of new relationships so she could grieve her divorce and find a way to focus on getting her financial life in order—those were top priorities. She admitted she gets hooked on men and what they feel about her. When she's dating, she's also prone to shopping for new clothes. I asked her to avoid clothing stores and she was finding it much harder to do than she realized.

I told her to consider consulting with a certified credit counselor or financial coach for some more in-depth and concrete strategies to handle her debt and current living expenses. I also asked her to continue to attend Debtors Anonymous, focus on generating more income, organizing her home and office, and watching her eating and exercise.

She began making progress. She also reported that her short-lived interest in the man at her dance classes had faded when he backed away. "I was really into him and he backed away. I felt sad. It reminded me of my husband. I have difficulty not getting what I want." It seemed that Rose was in many ways powerful but still had the core of a little girl: vulnerable, insecure and easily disappointed.

I believed Rose had some relationship addiction issues. She shared: "When these powerful men want me, I seem to push them away. Yet, I feel empowered when they adore me. When a woman feels that way, she can do anything." I asked: anything except take care of her finances?

Rose also had a side of her that was deeply religious and traditional. She believed, somewhere deep inside, that it was okay to cede her power to a man. Without preaching or making her wrong, I could see she was going be a challenge.

During the course of our therapy, Rose had to travel across the country for a family gathering due to someone's grave illness. The trip helped put things in perspective. First, the drama around her men issues and her finances paled in comparison to her family member who was fighting for her life. Second, it was an opportunity for her to observe and witness the family interactions and dynamics in a way she hadn't been able to before.

She noticed her thoughts and feelings: *"My family is very, very wealthy—there are many millionaires. I feel so poor and unloved when I'm there. I'm aware how I'm happy with who I am in all other respects except my money and finances. I shouldn't be in this situation. I'm so mad at myself. I can't sink. I've done so much work on myself. I think I've felt like I've deserved these things I've gotten used to—this lifestyle."*

She also noticed strong urges to shop while with family for a prolonged period of time. She relayed how a comment from her father made her feel "abandoned" and how she found herself at Saks Fifth Avenue where she bought some clothing and a book. While she didn't spend a fortune, it was clearly a triggered relapse into old, automatic behavior.

Upon her return home, Rose continued to see the man from her dance class. Despite my hints of caution, she persisted. She went to her 3rd Debtors Anonymous meeting and was encouraged to track her expenses in writing each day. She noticed she was still spending too much—mostly on things to make her feel beautiful and also on gifts for others. She even talked about needing to take a spiritual retreat to help her get centered. I suggested she find a very economical retreat and use it, in part, to meditate on her unhealthy patterns—financial and relational—and her new emerging life—rather than just an escape from reality. She found one.

When she returned from the retreat, she had obtained some further insights about herself. *"I notice that I don't tend to binge shop when I'm scared—when I'm scared I tend to become immobilized. It's when I feel safe, content, or excited that I tend to want to shop."* I told her that's a good insight but also to see how she recently went shopping when she felt abandoned and overwhelmed during her visit with family.

Rose finally broke up with the man she'd been dating. She concluded he was trying to use her and, frankly, she knew she was trying to use him. "I want to live life more fully," she asserted. She discovered that, somewhere in her thinking, she associated living life more fully with buying and having things, this lifestyle, and with being in relationship with a man. She seemed to know that this belief wasn't necessarily true—but it still seemed hard to abandon.

Rose then got a call from her ex-husband about something—they hadn't talked in quite a while. Hearing his voice opened up all kinds of memories and grief. He said he was happy with his life and was in a new relationship. *"I feel really bad, jealous, and sad. I was always hoping for another chance. I did spend a little because I was so upset but, at the same time, I could barely shop. I'm not even excited about spending money right now. I feel like a zero."*

There was a long pause. Then some important issues came up. "When I was young, around 19, I got pregnant and had an abortion and my significant other committed suicide shortly afterwards. I've never told my family about this. Afterwards, I was never able to get pregnant. I miss not being able to have children. It took me so many years to get over this guy. My heart was closed for a long time. Then I went out with another guy who used and manipulated me and betrayed me. This was all before I was in debt. I also realize my father was so focused on making money, saving

63

money, investing money that he never really spent any time with me or taught me anything—he didn't even teach me about money. I can remember two times when I was depressed that he tried to comfort me."

What connection do you see between these events and the initiation of your shopping and spending behaviors? I asked.

"I'm not sure," Rose said. "But it seems like I was trying to soothe myself or fill some void. I also need to stop worrying about my appearance so much even though I'm getting older and live in this appearance-obsessed environment. I also have to learn to speak up for myself. I really need to have a heart to heart with my father and get over this fear of him."

Rose struggled to connect the dots of her life. In the meantime, she stopped going to her local Debtors Anonymous meetings—something was always coming up on that night. I challenged her on this and also encouraged her to connect by phone with a holistic financial advisor to get some more concrete skills and strategies to deal with her debt—which she did do. My main goal had always been to help her stop the bleeding and to recognize where her patterns had come from.

Rose missed another Debtors Anonymous meeting and, instead, went out with a friend to buy quilts. "All my friends are shopaholics," she asserted. I met another friend recently at Neiman Marcus. *I guess I really need to view this shopping thing like recovery from alcohol."*

Now you're starting to get it, I said.

Rose set some goals: collect money owed from clients, generate new business, call credit card companies to transfer debt to lower interest cards, and pay her back property taxes. Within a week or so, she attained these goals. She noted that her depression lifted a bit and she felt a rush and a sense of accomplishment from following through with her actions.

The holiday season was fast approaching and we worked to have her limit her spending and to focus on the joys of the holidays. *"I need to focus more on God than things."* We also talked about using the New Year as a fresh start and a time of renewal. Her birthday was around the corner as well and she felt conflicted about what to buy for herself. It was a big birthday and she felt she deserved something nice. She verbalized *"the biggest present would be not buying anything."* She ended up buying a dress for $1,800. "It's worth it… and I've already worn it."

As we proceeded toward the end of our 10th session together, some progress had been made but Rose had a long way to go. She gained some tools and support systems for helping her curtail her shopping and spending—she just had to use them consistently. She gained some deeper awareness and insights into what has been driving her to over-shop and overspend: loneliness, low self-esteem, anger, emptiness, and difficulty resisting the culture of consumerism all around her. She also had moved from a place of fear of telling her father the truth about her financial failings to preparing to have a heart to heart with him in the near future.

During our 30-day follow-up appointment, Rose shared that she remained in a bit of a holding pattern. She acknowledged less fear around having a heart-to-heart with her father but still had not done so. She felt like she still didn't have the tools to stop shopping but also continued to work toward paying down her debt and avoiding shopping as best as she could.

Change takes time. The client needs to learn patience. So, too, does the therapist.

Notes & Reflections:

Mike and Susie's Story—The Compulsive Shopper

Mike and Susie are a couple in their late 40's who are struggling with a multitude of marital issues, most notably Mike's fairly recent descent into over-shopping and overspending—particularly online—since stopping drinking and going on disability from his work. They have a daughter with special needs. They've been divorced and remarried and were on the brink of divorce again.

I just finished working recently with Mike and Susie after nearly a year and a half of phone counseling together. They were some of my longer-term clients. In their late 40's, they had been married for about 15 years, divorced for a short time, and re-married. They have a daughter in her early teens with emotional and psychological challenges.

Susie contacted me after an Internet search. She sought help for her husband who, she was convinced, had a shopping and spending problem—mostly on e-Bay. He was also hoarding. Mike was diagnosed with bi-polar disorder and was a recovering alcoholic but, in reality, more of a dry drunk.

My first session was with Susie alone. I helped clarify why Mike may have gone off the deep-end recently. First, we noted that they had inherited money from Susie's mother and this created a false sense of financial security. Second, Mike had been physically and psychiatrically disabled and not working for the past few years—he had a lot of time on his hands and was felt restless and purposeless. Third, since Mike stopped drinking and hadn't adopted a recovery program, it was likely he had transferred his addictive-compulsive tendencies into shopping and spending. Fourth, the increasing stress of raising a daughter with special needs factored into Mike's wanting to escape. Finally, his mother's declining health and the anticipatory grief of her demise weighed upon him and began to morph into a power struggle with his wife, Susie, particularly over finances. Some call it: the "you're not my mother" syndrome.

According to Susie, Mike had spent nearly $200,000 in the last 2-3 years on computers and computer equipment—"for what, I don't know" she exclaimed. He, apparently, had some big project he wanted to accomplish but it never came to fruition. Their house, according to Susie, was all cluttered from Mike's equipment. I thought Mike might be going through a manic episode with delusions of grandiosity and suggested this to Susie. She stated that was possible even though Mike was taking his bi-polar meds.

What's he spending his money on now? I asked. "Now he's got this new project—he's gotten into Ham radios and he wants to build this big antennae tower in our backyard for broadcast and signal reception."

I was reminded of an old saying: "The difference between men and boys is the price of their toys."

I again suggested to her Mike may be having manic episodes, had transferred addictions, or was going through a mid-life crisis of sorts and was desperately struggling to find some meaning and challenge in his life since being disabled and out of work. I also explained that hoarding often occurs when people feel insecure or lost so they begin to focus on and hold onto things to ground them. All this made sense to her. The key was to have Mike understand it and, further, to find a way to engage him and interrupt the cycle so he could find some balance in his spending and in his soul.

I asked Susie if Mike would be open to having a session with me and her. She said she thought he might but she warned me: "he has good defense mechanisms and goes off on tangents a lot. He's hard to pin down." I later spoke by phone with a financial advisor of theirs who wished me good luck but didn't hold out much hope of progress given what she described as Mike's intractability.

I'll take my chances, I said.

Our first session was like a bullfight. I proceeded with caution by sharing with Mike that his wife had found me on the Internet and that I specialized in helping people—or couples—who are having money or spending issues. I stated it's not uncommon—that it's the most common issue of conflict in relationships. Mike roared out of the gate: "I'm entitled. I didn't get what I wanted when I was 14."

Not knowing Mike at all, I didn't know if he was serious, kidding, or testing me. When I asked him about his recovery from alcoholism, he stated bluntly: "A.A. makes me relapse." For a moment, I felt like the exorcist in the movie of the same title.

I back-tracked and asked them how they met. Susie started and Mike seemed quiet but began to slowly chide in. She talked about how they met, fell in love, and had a lot in common at one point. Mike shared more about his work life. He had worked in building and construction most of his life. So, it made sense that he needed to have some project to keep him busy and that he was having a hard time not working: his sense of identity as the breadwinner and as the strongman was greatly diminished. Susie worked part-time sporadically but really took care of the house and their daughter when she wasn't in school.

I asked about their child. Mike made it clear he really never wanted to have children. Susie was quiet. I asked about their divorce and how they got back together. Susie said, actually, that she left him because of his drinking and his spending—he was buying a lot of things for their house after inheriting some money. Susie said she was laid off her full-time job around this time, too. She moved out and Mike went downhill pretty quickly: he got a drunk-driving ticket and wound up in a psych ward.

Mike chimed in that once he stopped drinking he felt better and free. He tried to go back to college since he wasn't working but had trouble with information retention and test-taking. He did, however, stumble back into Ham radio and took some tests and did well with that. "I enjoyed Ham radio since I was 14." I asked him to explain what he meant when he had earlier stated he was entitled to spend what he wanted because he didn't get what he wanted when he was 14. He couldn't seem to elaborate. I suggested that's about the time most teen boys and girls really begin to rebel against mom or dad or authority in general.

I asked him what it was about Ham radio that he liked in the past and what attracted him to it now. "I enjoyed building everything by myself. I also enjoy the contacts you make with other Ham radio users. Lately, people are getting into things like bouncing signals off the moon or even communicating with the Space Shuttle and satellites. It's gotten very elaborate and, likewise, very expensive."

I saw an opening: Susie is more concerned about your finances that you are? Would you say that's accurate, Mike?

"I don't see it as so much of a problem. She just doesn't want me to spend any money or have any fun," Mike declared.

"We sat down with a financial planner in the last year and it doesn't look good. We've got very little retirement and a lot of medical issues between Mike and our daughter," Susie retorted.

"I've only spent about $20,000 on the Ham radio project and it's almost done," Steve protested. He then conceded a bit: "I like to build things. I probably have overspent and bought things I shouldn't have bought. I've got some of those items listed on e-Bay. I should be able to re-coup about $10,000."

"Mike tends to dive into projects that he hasn't planned out or budgeted for well and then has trouble completing them," Susie added.

"I don't deny that completely," Mike offered. "I do start things and when I run into problems, sometimes nothing gets done."

What is it you want from the other? I inquired.

Susie stated that she recognized Mike had already invested substantial time, energy and money into his project and that she understood his need to build things and be challenged, but she wanted him to understand that—given their financial situation—that his projects could be smaller scale—not as elaborate, expensive or, potentially, unable to be completed. She also wanted to know how much he was spending and a budget of what was still needed. She also wanted a reduction in clutter around the house. Finally, she needed to be able to trust him not to lie or deceive her about his expenditures.

For Mike's part, he wanted Susie's support in understanding why these projects were important to him and—given his years as the primary breadwinner—that he should be allowed some leeway to reward himself and play. He didn't want to be treated like a child or controlled.

How can we work together and reach a win-win here? I asked them. After a long pause, it was clear that this was something they had to think about a little more.

Mike and Susie agreed to work with me for 10 sessions— once a week—and to assess how things were going at the end of that period. Remembering that money issues aren't always just about money, I did some relationship building

71

exercises with them. I gave them an assignment to go out together at least one time a week—particularly when their daughter was in school. It didn't have to be complicated—a trip to Starbucks together would do. They could talk or just enjoy a ride together in silence.

I also asked each of them to say something he or she appreciated about the other. Susie, not surprisingly, went first. She admired Mike's intelligence, his conversation ability, his unique perspectives on things, and his ability to be sweet and loving to her and their daughter. Mike shared that he valued his wife's loyalty, upbeat temperament, her honesty, and her ability to forgive easily.

I have found that, sometimes, one needs to take a break from tackling a particular problem directly and get to it later, through the back door.

It became clear that the two reunited and re-married after Mike fell into a bad way. Susie was a classic co-dependent in many ways and came to his rescue as she was struggling financially and emotionally in her own way. Still, she had left Mike once before and she recognized that if he didn't stop his shopping and spending she might have to leave him again. While she used this threat as leverage, it wasn't effective in the face of a man who was out of control and who expressed deep ambivalence about the value of his life and of life in general.

"The whole ship is going down anyway," Mike was known to say. "The system's rigged. Our health insurance keeps going up. We'll probably never get all our debts paid off. Even with the inheritance and what we'll get when my Mom kicks the can, we'll barely be able to stay afloat. Why not have a good time while you can? I'm just trying to get what I want."

I could feel Susie's exasperation. "Well, I want enough money to support ourselves and our daughter and our retirement. There's no money left. You're the one causing this ship to go down. We had money at one time."

Suzie shared that they had received a $1million inheritance and a $400,000 home from her mother. They sold the home for $300,000 and had to pay-off the rest of the mortgage and taxes on the inheritance. Then, like a lot of people since 2001, they lost a lot of money in the stock market—nearly a half million. They had worked with a financial coach who helped them estimate that their living expenses alone ran $80,000 a year. Along with Mike's $200,000 computer project venture a few years back and what he was pumping into his current project, I could see how they would be out of money in the near future. Mike's mother gave him $500,000 to hold in a separate account. Susie was worried that Mike will dip into that money soon.

"It's too late to save money. It doesn't matter. We're all going down," Mike echoed.

It became clear to me that I needed to have a session just with Mike. Man-to-man—was my thinking. I was surprised he actually agreed.

Mike, tell me how you see yourself and your relationship with Susie.

"I have a negative worldview," Mike began. "I feel like Susie's never satisfied. If we broke up, I'd get a 40 foot yacht and get rid of most of all the other things. I don't have any energy anymore. All these medications sap my energy. It's like I'm a turtle moving in slow motion. I miss my manic episodes so much. I probably induce them with my projects.

"I believe in keeping some money for myself to use how I want it. Is that so wrong? Things aren't that bad—we've prepaid our daughter's college tuition and we prepaid for life insurance. So, if I die or she dies, we'll be set. She has no

confidence in me. The truth is: Susie was the only gal who seemed to like me. I've been with some crappy women. I finally thought: what would my Dad do? He would have loved Susie. She pursued me. I don't know where fate or karma is taking me. I don't know how to receive love. I don't even know how to love myself."

I felt Mike's vulnerability and resisted the temptation to pounce on him with an agenda to get him to change his behavior. I was sensitive to taking sides with his wife and pushing him further away. Instead, I explored his feelings.

It sounds like you feel defeated.

"Yeah, I guess that's how I feel at times—defeated."

What do you really want?

"I just want Susie's respect and trust back."

Do you think you can get that back? If so, how?

"I don't know. It seems like I've let her down too many times already."

I don't think so. I know you both have a heavy load in life but how would it be to work together as a team. Aren't you tired of all the fighting and mistrust? It doesn't have to be a winner-and-loser game. You need each other. And your daughter needs both of you.

Over the next few sessions, there was a noticeable shift in Mike's attitude and cooperation. He finally admitted he had a problem with out-of-control shopping and spending. I worked with him and Susie on concrete strategies and goals.

First, I asked Mike if it really was important to him to finish his Ham radio and tower project. He said it was. I managed to get both of them to agree to this but with some parameters.

Mike would need to allow Susie full access to his e-Bay account to monitor it and for them to get rid of one of their credit cards and monitor the use of the remaining card. I asked Mike to create a list of what items were already on order for his project and how much he expected them to cost as well as a projected timeline and budget for the remaining project—to be completed with decent quality but within reasonable cost. Then there was the issue of clutter around the house. They both agreed something needed to be done about that. They would each focus on a particular area and offer each help if needed. The goal was to figure out what could be thrown out, what could be donated, what could be sold on e-Bay or elsewhere, and what would be kept.

As I coached the couple, both sounded excited to be working together again as a team—with some common goals. The only question was whether they would follow through. They also arranged for a modest family vacation which, while it would cost some money, felt like a good idea from a therapeutic standpoint. I felt encouraged that they organized something together and could understand how they needed to get away from home, have some fun and rejuvenation before embarking on a very crucial chapter in their lives.

The couple ended up having a great trip and we continued to work on a bi-weekly basis for accountability on progress. Over the next year, there were ups and downs and times of moving forward and falling back. But we stayed steady.

One pivotal event came toward the end of that year when I recorded a few episodes of A&E TV's "Big Spender" and mailed the video to Mike and Susie. These half-hour segments featured an interventionist working with various compulsive shoppers and spenders. Two of the episodes featured male "shopaholics"—one who continued to be in denial about his problem (to the chagrin of his girlfriend) and another who really seemed to get how out of control he was and what it was doing to his wife. Both Mike and Susie found these helpful to watch. Mike, especially, could relate.

Even so, Mike continued to have periodic lapses with overspending and lack of communication. They were less severe and less frequent but Susie had become much more adept at discovering them and addressing them immediately. Mike tended to chalk these events up to forgetfulness rather than any intent to deceive. Susie had learned to address the issues directly and without shaming or drama. At the same time, she'd also learned to compliment, praise and acknowledge when Mike did something well. Overall, she saw progress on his honesty, his curtailing of spending, his progress on his Ham radio project, and his clearing of a substantial amount of clutter.

It's possible that, after staying on top of Mike's spending for over a year, he became worn down—tired of playing cat-and-mouse and more enthusiastic about working together and actually completing his project than about rebelling against Susie or proving he couldn't be controlled. Mike had moved toward being an equal partner in the marriage and not "a kid to be bossed around." Susie felt like she could work with him now. While they didn't always see eye-to-eye on everything, they developed the ability to listen better and to express their respective opinions promptly and directly. They also learned to compromise. Finally, they began to work together more evenly on the care of their daughter whose challenges had increased.

Mike and Susie have a long journey ahead. But they worked hard to break through their stalemate and near-divorce. I doubt I'll see Mike at any Debtors Anonymous—much less Alcoholics Anonymous—meetings anytime soon. But I do wish him and his family joy, satisfaction, and financial security and balance. They know they can call me anytime they need support or guidance.

Notes & Reflections:

Joyce's Story—The Compulsive Spender

Joyce is a middle-aged psychotherapist, married with children, who recently came to terms with her chronic overspending. Not so much an over-shopper as an overspender, she sought out both counseling and financial advising to help her discover the roots of her problems and how to get her life back on track. Note: Joyce was not a client of mine but someone who kindly agreed to contribute.

I'm 39 years old, almost 40, and have been married 7 years. We have two young children. I'm a psychotherapist and consider myself more of an over-spender than an over-shopper. Still, it's embarrassing. I live on the East Coast where everything is pretty expensive—the cost of living is pretty high. Most of my overspending has been on things like food and going out to eat. I racked up about $20,000 in credit card debt over a 4 year period.

I would say my overspending began when I was first out on my own—when I began graduate school, around the age of 24. My parents paid for college and I worked, mostly for "play money." I spent mostly on going out to restaurants— we generally went Dutch, so I mostly spent it on myself. I admit: I've always been an emotional eater and struggle with my weight a bit.

I have had therapy for other issues but not necessarily for money or spending issues. It took me a few years of overspending in college before I realized I had a problem—that I had credit card bills I couldn't pay off on time. I borrowed money from a relative to pay off the bills and paid them back over time but I still didn't really recognize at the time that it was an issue I needed to sort through.

I didn't grow up around much spending—my parents were pretty conservative in their spending. *But there were some confusing messages around money. Growing up, my folks would say things that implied they were fairly well off yet they were reluctant to spend money on me and my siblings and sometimes gave the impression they could not spare it.*

I think my overspending—at least a big part of it—relates to my relationship with my parents and the relationship between financial resources and emotional resources. I very much linked the two together. I have not always been able to see certain aspects of my parents as they really are and I think that has parallels for me in my management of money. For example, I have sometimes made unwise financial decisions, not taking adequate responsibility for getting clear on what I really had and what I really could afford with the hopes that things would just work out somehow. *I think it is also about my ambivalence about really growing up and taking ownership of my life.*

My family knows a bit about our debt but it is not something we discuss often. My husband didn't know much about my spending issues or debt when we were dating and at the time of our marriage because it was somewhat subtle and I mostly managed the money. Most of my spending is on small stuff but of course, it adds up. When my husband and I finally confronted our debt—my debt—he was somewhat angry. Still, it took us both a pretty long time to get serious about fixing this. I have to say that the thing that has helped me most get this under control has been our work with our financial planner. She has been very gentle yet firm about the seriousness of the situation and somehow, hearing it from her was a wake-up call for me.

We are now using a system where all of our income goes into one account which we have set up to give us a set amount each month to live on. We have consolidated our debt and no longer use credit cards. *It is embarrassing that I have gotten myself into this situation—I am a well-educated professional who "should know better."* It will take us quite a while to pay off the debt but at least we have a plan that we are sticking to in order to move things forward. We are moving in the right direction.

Notes & Reflections:

Part Two

The Bigger Picture

Through my research, my own personal recovery, and my work with clients—and in my two previous books—I distilled some of the most common psychological reasons people shoplift, commit employee theft, or other kinds of theft. I believe the motivations are relatively similar in regards to compulsive shopping or spending—or to most other addictions for that matter.

TOP TEN REASONS PEOPLE OVER-SHOP/OVERSPEND

1. Grief and Loss, To Fill the Void
2. Anger/Life is Unfair, To Get Back/Make Life Right
3. Depression, To Get a Lift
4. Anxiety, To Comfort
5. Acceptance/Competition, To Fit in
6. Power/Control, To Counteract Feeling Lost/Powerless
7. Boredom/Excitement, To Live on the Edge
8. Shame/Low self-esteem, To Be Good at Something
9. Entitlement/Reward, To Compensate for Over-giving
10. Rebellion/Initiation, To Break into Own Identity

If you've read the stories in the first part of this book, you have likely identified many of the above reasons people stumble into compulsive shopping and spending. As with any addiction, nobody starts off planning to get out of control. Nobody starts off intending to get into debt, lie, hide purchases, or become obsessed with shopping, spending money, or with things. It happens a little at a time. It's insidious. Our culture conspires to create "supercomsumers" out of all of us.

Some of us, especially, are more vulnerable to addictive-compulsive behaviors based on a variety of factors: biology or genetics (chemical imbalances in our brains); psychological/personality traits such as being perfection-minded, control-oriented, passive-aggressive, or impatient; sociological influences such as role modeling, peers, culture, ethnicity; and religious/spiritual conditioning—such as being taught not to want, poverty is holy or to live in fear due to rigid beliefs or to have a total absence of religious or spiritual guidance. This theory is called the "bio-psycho-social-spiritual" theory of addiction.

Within the bio-psycho-social-spiritual theory is the essence of what I believe prompts us to act: beliefs. We develop and adopt beliefs throughout our lives which become our truths. These beliefs can easily fuel over-shopping or overspending. An example is the simple belief that if I look good (or better) people will like me better. Now, one may believe this to a small degree and not have it translate into behavior that will hijack one's life. But most people are unconscious of their thoughts or they may be prone to "stinking thinking."

All behavior—whether freely chosen or stemming from an addictive mind set—originates from our beliefs which are made up of thoughts and, also, values—which are also sub-sets of beliefs and values. Our values come from our families, our peers, our culture—both ethnic and national, our media, and elsewhere. Often, we find ourselves holding conflicting values such as a value toward honesty and hard work and a competing value of finding the loopholes and the shortcuts to the easier job.

Compulsive Shoppers

We've been using the phrase "compulsive shopper" throughout the book. The classic compulsive shopper tends to shop to avoid or suppress a core of pain—usually from trauma or loss. The compulsive shopper may shop fairly consistently or become triggered by something and then go shopping as an automatic response to distract from painful or uncomfortable emotions.

Trophy Shoppers

Trophy shoppers tend to need to be the best at everything and, thus, to have the best of everything. The trophy shopper—regardless of income level—seeks to find the perfect accessory for outfits, high end items—be they art, furniture, clothes, and—often—the more rare or hard to find, the better.

Image Shoppers

Image shoppers are similar to trophy shoppers on the surface because they tend to buy nice things, too. Their motivation is different, however. The image shopper buys things less for the inherent value of the items themselves and more for the image those items project to others. The image shopper needs to impress others more than the trophy shopper does.

Bargain Shoppers

Bargain shoppers are driven by the need to get a good deal—regardless of income level. It boosts their mood, their self-esteem and symbolically soothes their pervasive feeling of being shortchanged in some area of their lives. They often buy things they don't need but feel are too hard to pass up.

Codependent Shoppers

Codependent shoppers primarily buy things for other people to gain love and approval and to keep others from leaving or abandoning them. They feel their primary worth or value is what they can give to others.

Bulimic Shoppers

Bulimic shoppers are sometimes referred to as "binge shoppers." They may have relatively short or episodic outbursts of excessive shopping—usually during times of stress. Bulimic shoppers—like bulimic eaters—may also engage in a pattern of "bingeing and purging": shopping and then returning the items almost immediately after purchase; the initial buying is cathartic but then guilt or ambivalence sets in so the returning also brings relief.

Collector Shoppers

Collector shoppers are similar to trophy shoppers in that they typically are focused more on attaining or accumulating items for personal satisfaction rather than to impress others. Unlike trophy shoppers, collector shoppers don't necessarily have to possess the best or hard to find items; rather, the collector shopper typically becomes obsessed with having complete sets of something to feel empowered or in control. Collector shoppers are often hoarders.

Spenders vs. Shoppers

There are people who are less concerned with "things" than experiences or who may make occasional—rather than frequent—purchases are financially excessive. Overspenders may splurge on dining out, vacations, theater and concerts, hosting parties, weddings, or gatherings, or may exceed their budget on cars, homes, an engagement ring, or other "lifestyle" purchases.

Natasha Kendal, PhD

Dr. Kendall is a friend and colleague of mine in the Detroit area who has a specialty in working with money issues with couples and families. She was generous to sit down with me for an in-depth interview.

I'm a marriage and family therapist who has a degree in marriage and family therapy from Michigan State University. When I was working on my dissertation, I chose the subject of couples and money deliberately because I really wanted to find that intersection between couples and marital satisfaction and the money piece.

Most of us know how money plays a big part in any marriage as it pertains to marital dissatisfaction. We've all heard that money conflicts are the number one reason for conflict and divorce—if you open up any magazine, that's what they talk about. *But in the professional literature—for therapists—there's very little about money and relationships.* It's almost like it's a taboo. So, I really wanted to explore this intersection of money and relationships because it seemed like a vital but underdeveloped area.

I've done many interviews where I've asked people what they think about how money affects their relationships. *I have discovered a lot of money dysfunction and compulsivity.* When I think about compulsive behaviors, the first thing I think about is addiction. Addiction is a disease that has ramifications not just for the individual but for the couples' relationship as well as for the whole family.

As a couples and family therapist, I am always approaching any problem from a couples or family perspective. In my work, I often go into people's homes to interview them there and to see, firsthand, what's going on in terms of where the money may be going. I work with children and adolescents, too.

Culture also plays into attitudes about money but I tend to focus on family culture rather than ethnic culture. I'm more concerned with the messages about money and spending received by children as they grew up.

However, I can tell you as a person of Russian descent who came to the U.S. over 20 years ago that, in Russia, this issue of over-shopping or overspending wasn't an issue 15-20 years ago. The culture wasn't reared to be materialistic. It was very much into family, work, and survival above everything. However, I think that this "acquisition hunger" is in every human being because when the Russian culture changed in the early '90's—from what I've heard from family and friends who still live there and from what I've read as well—the materialism absolutely exploded.

You will see this happen virtually anywhere a country switches over from a communist or socialist dictatorship to a more capitalist system. Look at China and you'll see this beginning to happen as well. You'll find people becoming very money oriented and materialistic.

So, I believe that there's this kind of hunger in all of us—it's just a matter of containing it. It's not so much based on national origin as on the opportunities that people do or do not have.

In my work of late, I can think of a family where the husband is a businessman and the wife stays home with the three children. The dynamic of the family is such that the husband would be gone for many days on end, come home for a couple or nights, and then be gone again. The wife truly felt very isolated, neglected and overwhelmed. The only difference between her and a single mother was that she had a very cushy account. Her roles in the family—taking care of the children, the home, and the pets—were also undervalued.

So, she desired to soothe herself and to reclaim her power. She felt like she needed to shop to empower herself. The children would be at school during the day and she would spend inordinate amounts of time shopping. The area she focused on was home decorations, making her home beautiful. She also focused on her children's needs like clothing—not her own clothing. She even felt virtuous about this: "Look what I'm doing? I'm doing this for others."

Really, the problem started to rear its ugly head over time as the husband, who would come home every now and then, opened the credit card statements. He would be just appalled at the amount of money it would take to run the household. *He couldn't understand how or why she spent so much and didn't realize that, beneath everything, this was a power issue. She felt so out of control and so disempowered in the marriage that this is how she chose—very unconsciously, mind you—to exercise power.*

The phone call for help actually came from the mother. The presenting problem we started with was the children's behavior. They were out of control. *Very often that's how couple's issues come to my attention—through a referral from a teacher or a school social worker or somebody who works with one or all of the children. Children often act out the problems of their parents or their families.* Again, in this case, the children were fighting and disobeying—there was a lot of disrespectful behavior toward the mother. That's how it often manifests. We worked together on multiple fronts—with the kids, with the marriage.

I've coined and trademarked this term *"financial crucible."* It is really a parallel to a very well-known term in psychology called "the sexual crucible." The financial crucible, like the sexual crucible, relies on the premise that one can look at and heal the entire relationship through working on one aspect of it, one window. If it's been accepted in the realm of the sexual, why can't we focus on the realm of the financial?

All of the key dynamics in couples and groups play themselves out in the financial arena. There are five principle areas that are noteworthy:

1. *power and control*
2. *trust and mistrust*
3. *commitment*
4. *belonging*
5. *caring*

If we can discuss these aspects as they relate to money and spending, we can use them as a window into fully understanding the dynamics of the relationship and better determine how to heal that relationship.

Let me give some examples that really illustrate this. This also comes from a book called "You Paid How Much for That?" *Commitment is a very common area of fighting.* However, couples won't always understand that it is the commitment issues that they are fighting about—what I call "the hidden issues."

Commitment is a very common issue in second and subsequent marriages because one of the spouses will often feel that the commitment isn't there—whether it's physical, emotional, sexual, or financial. They may be fighting about a stepchild's dance classes and the argument may be over the money or the use of time but, in reality, the hidden issue is how much money is being allocated to the stepchild vs. the couple's relationship—so, commitment. Is it really about the money or something else?

Let's look at *belonging.* I was working with a family where a husband came from a large, very wealthy family where wealth was passed on from generation to generation. The wife came from a more modest background. She really could not understand what was wrong but she was feeling kind of awkward and uncertain inside, kind of left out. When we talked, it occurred to me that the issue may be—as they say in Britain—"either you're born to the manor or you're not." And she was not "born to the manor." She was not related to her husband by blood. Did she belong to that subculture or not?

Now interestingly, she felt treated inclusively in the social circles, the clubs, on the ski slopes where they vacationed. "Everyone welcomes me—I feel like I'm part of the community" but not to her husband. She was "not to the manor born." It played itself out where her husband eventually said to her: "this is not your money. I don't care if we've been married for years. It's my money and I will do whatever I wish with it." There were very clear financial boundaries. We worked on this; sometimes it's irresolvable.

Another example is one about *caring*. Anyone with a background in financial services should recognize this. Very often, one partner in a couple has a very large life insurance policy on his life. This is usually the breadwinner—for if he passed away, the insurance would help fill in for the missed income. However, couples rarely think about getting life insurance on a spouse who doesn't work or who works part-time even though if you went out and tried to replace that spouse's services—which typically are home-centered—it would cost tens of thousands of dollars per year. So, again, it's a financial issue and there will still be major ramifications if either spouse dies.

It, therefore, becomes an issue of not caring enough about the contributions of the other spouse. I'd say American culture is guilty of focusing mostly on the monetary contributions of a partner or family member. An example I like to use is that of pets. Pets are often very valued in a family. But what is the financial contribution of a pet:

nothing. If anything, they cost money. Yet, we feel that they contribute. It's the same with kids—up to a certain point.

So, these are some of the issues I look at through the "financial crucible." Every couple has issues that are uniquely their own. *If we can isolate these issues through the lens of money and the relationship to money, we can understand ourselves and heal the dysfunctional patterns.*

I also am fond of a term called *"polarization." Couples always become more polarized over time on a variety of matters due to lack of communication, recurring fights, and building of resentments.* In other words, if a couple starts off pretty close on an issue or value—say 49% to 51% in alignment—years of fighting and disagreements will force them to the opposite ends of the pole, like 5% to 95%.

Naturally, with any couple, one of the partners may have a leaning or tendency toward spending while the other has a leaning or tendency toward saving. As time goes on, each partner may fall into a habit of trying to compensate for the other's leaning or tendency—so the saver begins to save more as the spender spends and vice-versa. Things eventually get out of hand and kind of spiral.

The typical case is when a wife goes shopping and maxes out the credit card and the husband begins to lecture her about her spending and how they have to be very careful. Often he'll say we need to cut something out or cut down on their spending; typically, he'll start with the groceries. She'll often be resentful but will try to cut down for a few weeks and then, after a while, she'll begin to tell herself: "he's not realistic. The children have to eat." She'll then overspend even more as if to make a point about how much things really cost. So, now it's a month later, and there's a confrontation because he feels she didn't keep to the agreement. "Why didn't you keep to the agreement?" he'll ask. She'll call him unreasonable. He'll call her a spendthrift.

Month after month after month this pattern will continue. It's very insidious. Now she's spending more because she feels he doesn't care about her. Soon, there becomes lies and hiding—on both parts. She may hide her purchases from him—maybe she'll even turn to shoplifting. He may get a raise or a bonus from work and not tell her about it—just put it away somewhere so she can't spend it. Sooner or later these things become known and some serious trust issues ensue.

Another common pattern is when one partner feels controlled by money and doesn't feel like an equal, she may withhold sex or affection—often unconsciously—because she's feeling hurt or demeaned. Likewise, a partner may feel that he's being used or unappreciated. And these days, it doesn't have to be gender-specific.

I often try to remind couples that there's hope. I remind them that when they started out they were not so far apart and maybe they've drifted a bit but they really aren't that far apart if they can figure out their real concerns. I tend to do brief therapy with most of my couples where I assess and evaluate them intensively over 3 weeks, we work on the issues for six weeks, and then we have a follow-up typically on the 10th week.

I'd also like to say a little more about my work with children and money. It's such an important topic, especially as it relates to *overindulgence. It's amazing how children are educated or, rather, not educated about money. Parents overindulge their kids into learning to be excessively materialistic. Often, parents make up their shortcomings through buying their kids things.* Children, by nature, are fabulous consumers: they want everything they see, they're indiscriminate. They want that and they want that and they want that. And then they want some more. And if their friend has one of those, they have to have one of those.

Freud was right about kids: initially, they have nothing but an "id." What they really want is *everything* they want. And that is a very natural human tendency for a child, to want what he wants without any breaks or restrictions. So, children are also fabulous victims for overindulgence. They want it all and no matter how much you give them they'll want more. You don't often hear a child say: "a third cookie? No, two is enough." He'll eat the third cookie and throw up later.

So, this is an arena where parents have really found they can assuage their own guilt by buying things for their kids. It becomes kind of a comical part of our culture. It's like the businessman who comes home from a trip with a stuffed animal for his child because he feels bad he's left her, maybe missed her recital. He may do the same thing for his wife. And then he'll get into the pattern of bringing something home every single time. Then, when he comes through the door, the first greeting is: "hi Daddy, what did you get me?" And that becomes part of the family culture. So, Daddy becomes a "getter of things" rather than a father figure.

On the flip side—the mother's side—it is often very hard to balance family and career. We've been bombarded with the idea that we can have it all—perfect balance. Women, especially, try to work, clean the home, cook the perfect meal, and show up at the soccer games. Well, that's not humanly possible. So, a lot of mothers give in, just like the Dads, and overindulge their kids.

The feeling is: let's buy something, either an experience, or a toy or a gift, or a fabulous trip. All of this really adds up to dollars and cents. And time is a commodity. So, instead of taking a 3-week camping trip, we take a 4-day trip somewhere that costs the same. We aren't doing a great job of educating our kids who are the next generation of consumers.

Another interesting and challenging dilemma is that ours is the first generation who seems destined to not do as well financially as the previous generation. Generally, we're not doing as well as our parents and grandparents. This has to do with a lot of macro-economic issues. But for many individuals, and I've seen this in a lot of my patients, there is this feeling of inadequacy. It becomes harder to find good work, to have a nice house, to live in a nice neighborhood, to drive a nice car, to go on nice vacations. Or if we are able to swing this, we're doing so by going into a lot of debt. *We're working more and more and having this feeling of not getting ahead.*

This was not the case one generation ago. And many people feel frustrated, dumb-founded, and often blame themselves. It's "The American Way"—every generation is supposed to do better than the one before.

There's a book out there called "The Overspent American" and another one called "The Overworked American." And if you're working 50-60 hours a week, you're going to need to hire somebody to do some of the things you'd otherwise do if you had time—watch the kids, clean the car, mow the lawn, dry cleaning. We used to wash our own clothes, cook our own food, clean our own homes, and tend our own yards. We're paying for all these services that used to be done at home. It becomes a vicious cycle.

It's not only the hours we work in the office but outside the office, too. We answer the phones, e-mail, our Blackberrys, or we're thinking about work even when we're home. And kids—as well as our partners—sense this. *Then, of course, they feel unloved, unappreciated, and then they settle for toys and material things which never really fulfill our needs.* And as more things are bought and more money spent, we feel we need to work harder. Again, it's a vicious cycle.

The only thing I can say that is hopeful about this trend of over-shopping and overspending is that I feel we are waking up to these issues and also about the problems with overindulgence. So, there's a backlash beginning to happen. There is a movement toward simplicity that is growing.

For example, there's a group called "Birthdays without Headaches" where parents assist each other by throwing simple backyard birthday parties for their kids rather than the elaborate, expensive affairs. Let kids be kids and just enjoy each other. The 1980s were the epitome of excess and it's still taking some time to fade—even as other developing countries are ramping up their consumerism.

I think a lot of people are waking up. One thing I feel it's important for parents to teach their kids is that it's okay to be different. It's okay to stand out. You don't have to conform or dress like everyone else. You don't have to have what everyone else has. It's important for children as well as adults. It's pretty simple but we all really need to learn: I'm good enough.

Notes & Reflections:

Pamela Landy, JD, CFP

Ms. Landy has been a friend and colleague of mine for six years. She is also my wife's and my financial planner. We have learned invaluable information about money and finances from Ms. Landy and her associates. It is truly an evolving, lifelong education. Here's her interview with me.

Terry Shulman: What is your background and position?

Pamela Landy: I have a law degree and practiced law for a while but I have been a certified financial planner for approximately fifteen years. I work with a small fee only financial planning company with offices across the United States. Our focus is on middle-income clients.

TS: How prevalent is compulsive shopping and spending among your clientele?

PL: That's a very interesting question. I have a hard time telling you that because one of the problems we have is that most people know roughly how much they make and most of them know roughly how much they pay in taxes. However, most of them have no clue as to how much they spend. Usually, it takes quite a while of working with the client before they really either share the truth or even get a handle on what's going on—they're quite resistant to it. So, from this, I can only assume that it's a major problem.

There's such shame and secrecy around this. I'm not talking about just women either—because it's usually women I think we most readily think about with over-shopping or overspending—it's both men and women. I don't think I was fully aware of this issue, except for an occasional family member or friend, until I started doing more holistic financial planning and working with more people. I think that's what a lot of people fear in coming to a financial planner or advisor: opening up their insides—it's more sensitive than talking about sex or any other intimate topic. It seems to be more revealing.

TS: Can you give an example or two in your actual work?

PL: I can think of a couple. But, first of all, this issue comes up a lot. I have an example with a male—which is different than the norm. What happened was one of the spouses came in without the other and they were very friendly, talkative people, and the guy was sitting there and was talking about how he had a separate investment account where he had lost a lot of money gambling with stocks. He was very embarrassed about it and didn't want us to know about it. So, that's one situation with shame and secrecy around money.

We also have clients who want to keep certain accounts secret and not want us to look at them. That's usually an indication that there's something to hide. We've had several situations where couples do this when they're dating and they don't want to reveal certain information. As we counsel them together it becomes evident there's a huge amount of credit card debt coming into the marriage. It's a big issue.

Sometimes couples come to us after discovering on their own that there's this debt and they want help with it. We had one situation that became apparent before a couple got married where the woman had a spending problem and a prescription drug addiction. She had closets full of clothes with the tags still on them. We're talking tens of thousands of dollars of credit card debt—just from clothes and jewelry and not just because she needed these things but, it was obvious, she felt inadequate and empty and was trying to overcompensate and fill a void. It caused a lot of problems for the couple because the potential spouse was just they other way—he was very controlled in his spending and began to worry that he would enable her because he made a lot of money as a physician and could somewhat afford to subsidize her lifestyle. It becomes a relationship issue.

I think the healthiest couples we've seen are those who come to us while they are still dating to try to air out their money issues ahead of time to avert potential problems.

TS: Well, my wife and I came to work with you almost immediately after our marriage in 2002. Does that count?

PL: Yes, that was wise of you both—better late than never! I also have single clients who I see overspending tremendously because they think it's their due because they don't have a family. It seems like there's often a void in their lives. I have one client who is very able to secure a good retirement except that she's spending most of her money that should be going into retirement plans and other savings on her house—to the tune of about $100,000 a year. It's not that she shouldn't have a hobby or enjoy her home but I don't think she realizes the extent to which she's compromising her future. We haven't been able to persuade her to cut back at all—that this would allow her to have both a comfortable present and a secure future. In that respect, I look at this as a problem. I don't know what else we can do to convince her about the magnitude of her spending.

TS: Do you ever use the word "shopaholic" or explain to clients that their shopping or spending is compulsive and that they may need professional therapy or counseling beyond what a financial planner or advisor can offer?

PL: It's a delicate issue. We try not to use the term "shopaholic" or "spendaholic" but we do talk about the "high" that people get and we do say that, at its core, this is not just a financial issue but it's indicative of something else—voids or problems that people have—and it doesn't matter how well we teach you about money. Money is not the real problem—money problems are the result of some other problems. We do talk about that and we do sometimes refer them to counseling and when it's a couple we refer them to couples counseling because it becomes more of a relationship issue than a financial issue.

I think a lot of individuals and couples would benefit from a combination of both sound financial counseling and psychotherapeutic counseling.

Another example is when one partner overspends to get back at the other partner. It's anger-related. They use the spending as a weapon. They'll say "well, I'm just going to go out and spend money because I know it irks him... or her."

TS: What is your overall goal when working with your clients? Or, can you explain how you work holistically with them and toward what end?

PL: Our overall goal is to make sure people's spending is in alignment with their values. We spend time uncovering and assessing each individual's—or the couple's—values. We try to get some agreement on values and then help them try to reach goals that are consistent with those values. We help them learn the best strategies to achieve these goals and help keep them on track. They say you can tell a lot about a person by looking at how they spend money and what they spend it on. It's true but it's also true that sometimes people fall out of alignment with who they are and their core values. In our work, we try to have an in-depth conversation at least once a year about values. Then we go back and see if their behavior is in alignment with their values. We try not to be judgmental—that's another reason we do some values testing because we're aware that it's very easy to inject your own values into the situation.

TS: So, if you have someone who is a "bon vivant" or a "gambler" what do you do?

PL: Well, for instance, if someone does like to gamble—at least for fun or leisure, not pathologically—we might suggest they set up an account with a certain amount of money. It's their gambling account—whether it's for casino gambling or for something like buying certain stocks. As long as you can budget or limit yourself, then you don't have a problem.

TS: When people come to you they have some goal in mind, right? They want some kind of help with something.

PL: That's right. Sometimes they come to us with a very specific problem or goal but often they recognize they need ongoing education and direction in a number of areas—be it taxes, investing, money and relationship issues. Our holistic approach incorporates all of this under the broader goal of helping clients better understand and manage their money and, therefore, their lives. And it's never over. It's an evolving process. Typically, your values don't change but your goals do. We find that people who are out of control with their spending are usually out of alignment with their values so that when they do align their spending with their values things are much more manageable in their lives across the board. So, when they realize it's not an issue of depriving themselves or doing without but, rather, finding out where they really want to spend their money.

One of the things we often suggest is a cash management system. What we do is we have the individual or couple put all their income into one account—we call it a "working account." Then the monthly amount for household expenses is transferred out of that account into another account or directly drawn out of the account to pay the bills. The reason we do that is because people hate to budget or even deal with how much they are spending each month just to survive. But this is a real easy way we can get a grip on how much people are spending and they can, too. If we fill an account with $10,000 and then we set up the budget for automatic withdrawals to pay the bills, we'll find out real quick if people are spending more than they bring in because the bills won't get paid.

Somehow, this is an easier, less confronting way of giving someone a reality check. But what's been funny is that I've been encountering a lot of resistance from people in setting up this system. I think people don't want to know how much they're spending or they don't want a spouse to know how much they're spending. I had that happen just last week with a couple—they're both attorneys—and one said out loud: "I don't want to know what I'm spending!" I think she was afraid to know or afraid for her partner to know.

It's funny, because it's a decent system—I don't care about the details of what people are spending their money on or how much—as long as the bills are getting paid and there's enough left over for savings and retirement. We need to know and we want people to know what they're spending monthly so they can plan.

TS: Would you say you see more people living beyond their means than people who are—on the other hand—being too frugal or too conservative with spending money?

PL: I think it's 90/10. I'd say about 90% of the people we see are spending at least 10% more than they make. This is when they first come in—before we work with them. Then, about 10% of people may be living in too much fear about spending or losing money. Again, it's partly about values but it's also a generational thing.

The Depression Era people are, generally, those who are afraid to spend. Then you've got the babies, the children of those people, who are the opposite. So, to break it down, I'd say that 75% of the Depression Era folks are going to die with a substantial amount of money left over. This is a small percentage of our clients due to age and other factors. So, we do some work with them on how to let go of money—

through giving to charities, gifts to family members or others while they're alive rather than give it to them when they die.

Then the next generation after the Depression Era—the baby boomers—are about 50/50 in spending more than they make. Of course, this may not necessarily hurt them as they likely will receive inheritances from their Depression Era parents.

Then there's the younger group—the kids of the baby boomers—when they come in to work with us they are usually spending at least 10% more than what they make and our goal it to get them to save at least 10% of their income so it's a 20% swing. But that's what's really hard. The younger people are used to spending their money on fun and frivolous things rather than just living expenses and savings. A lot of them have an attitude of entitlement where they don't think they should have to spend their money on the basics and then that carries into marriage. Often, a couple may argue over who should pay for the basics and who should pay for the fun stuff. Rather, they need to pool their incomes and discuss their values and get some guidance in making sure they're in alignment with them.

The younger generation also has an expectation that they will receive an inheritance. They're just praying and thinking that some inheritance will solve all their money issues—even though they wouldn't know how to deal with it if they did get it. That's a very common syndrome. Money doesn't solve all problems.

TS: Can you say something about this phenomenon of "time is money" thinking, of people spending money to save time?

PL: I actually see this in a lot of clients but also saw this when I was a practicing attorney. Anyone who bills for their time has ingrained in them the belief that time equals money. When time is money and you feel you have no time, you think that if you spend more money you'll have more time automatically. It doesn't necessarily work that way though.

Attorneys are some of the worst overspenders there are. First, they don't usually like to work in finances—they tend to be more verbal—but also they feel like their time is money so they justify buying things or overspending based on the fact that they don't have the time—they'll buy all these gadgets—anything they think is going to save them time. They'll spend extra money on all kinds of services—from eating out to dry cleaning to paying somebody to fix something they could do on their own. When they go on vacation—if they go at all—they tend to splurge because they think "I don't know when I'm going to go on vacation again or if I'll ever get one." They feel entitled because they are overworked but then all their overspending becomes a vicious cycle because then they need to work more to afford their overspending. And it's not just attorneys. A lot of people have the same pattern and dilemma.

The other thing we see is that because there's such a taboo against talking about money a lot of parents don't teach their kids enough about money—no matter what generation you are. So, the kids have to learn on their own or learn the hard way by making mistakes. An encouraging sign is that some of our clients are sending their kids to us to teach them about money issues through meetings that we have. There's also more out there in terms of books, articles, and other education materials for teaching kids about money. So, that's a good trend.

The problem is that many in the younger generation continue to be money-focused or stuff-focused. They basically equate everything with money and stuff and there's this sense of entitlement. You see it in all classes—lower, middle, upper—this sense of entitlement is scary. They don't realize what it took to make the money. They take for granted what they have and they're not realistic about the next steps it's going to take to get further ahead. They expect somebody to give them it right off the bat.

TS: Have you read or heard that the current generation—the younger generation—may be the first generation to have less than the previous one?

PL: Yes, and this scares me because as the parents of this generation become older and more vulnerable I think there's going to be a lot of elder abuse and financial abuse by this younger generation not learning how to make and manage money well and that they'll feel entitled to manipulate or take what they want. I just don't know how it's going to change based on how things are now. The cultural messages are so strong. The best thing parents can do is not give their children too much and also to teach them about money.

TS: Can you say something about divorce or bankruptcy as it relates to your clients?

PL: Well, first of all, we don't encourage bankruptcy because we've found it's very damaging beyond how it affects your credit. It's emotionally damaging to people. It's something I think we should teach our children. In most cases, I'd say it's better for a person or a couple to fight their way out of bankruptcy for the sake of their psyche and their future than erasing the problems. One of the issues is that if you don't cure the underlying issue or end the psychological or financial habits you're going to be right back there again. A huge percentage of people who go through one bankruptcy go through another one as soon as they can. It's the same thing with divorce. They just do the same thing again.

There are certain circumstances where we would recommend bankruptcy and have recommended it—like when a bankruptcy is caused by sudden and uncontrollable events like medical problems, disability, and sometimes divorce— something where it's not a systemic ongoing problem that is likely to repeat itself. That can give people a fresh start and that is what the bankruptcy rules were meant to address. We do have clients who have been bankrupt and they understand the need for a financial planner if they realize they need to learn a new way to live. It's kind of like being in recovery from an addiction. The downside of bankruptcy is it stays on your record for 7 to 10 years and it can prevent you from doing certain things.

One can successfully recover from bankruptcy but it depends on how you approach it: is it a cleansing that helps you create a fresh start and a new way of approaching money or is it a trick to get you out of a jam that you're just going to end up creating all over again because you think there are no consequences?

As for divorce, we do encounter that quite a bit since 50% of marriages end in divorce. Divorce can be one of the most devastating events financially and emotionally that can occur in a person's life. Despite some cases of one partner gaining a lot through divorce, more likely it is financial ruin or, at least, some form of starting over at square one. One, your assets are now split in half. Two, you're often running two households instead of one. Three, if you have children, you're likely to spend more on your children to buy their affection or to assuage your guilt or to compete with the other parent. Then, of course, there's paying your lawyers. Also, splitting your other assets like your retirement plans—all of the sudden, you only have half. Divorce reminds me of that game Chutes and Ladders—when you get a chute you have to go back. So, divorce can be like going back to age 30 when you're 50.

TS: What do you think of the financial advisors in the media like Suze Orman and others?

PL: I think Suze Orman has good advice because she does a lot of work with the psychology of money. Some of them, like Jim Cramer, talk more about stocks than other issues. Dave Ramsey is good because he talks about the whole philosophy and mindset of "no debt." He understands that it's not just about spending money, that there are a lot of emotions behind spending money. I actually think the ones who address the underlying issues are good. They may not always have the same philosophy and their services may be different but I think they're contributing to the awareness around money and giving them a track to run on as it pertains to dealing with money.

I would encourage people to approach money like they approach their health. Of course, many people don't approach their health well so this may not register how I'm intending it to. Look at your money history just like you or a doctor would look at your health history. What are the pieces that formed you? What are the money "genetics" you inherited from your parents in terms of attitudes? What else or who else has influenced you? Where are your preconceived ideas coming from? How can you develop skills and knowledge to counteract the things that are "genetic" to you? I think I'd encourage people to work on their money like they might work on their health to improve their overall quality of life and their happiness.

TS: Do you see that, generally, people who take care of their health take care of their money or vice-versa?

PL: I definitely see when people are not taking care of their health it shows up in their money because for some reason— maybe it's the energy of money—when you have no energy for health reasons you seem to not be able to deal with money at all. I see a strong correlation with that. I've seen that a lot and feel very strongly about this. In terms of the other way, there are plenty of people I know who are in good health but don't deal with money very well but for many, it's just a matter of time before their money issues end up affecting their health.

Notes & Reflections:

Excerpts of Recent Newspaper Articles of Interest

Frugality Can Be Acquired, but It Can't Be Bought
New York *Times*, March 1, 2008
By Caitlyn Kelly

Consumers, long held up as the saviors of the American economy as it rose, are taking some of the blame for its fall. Consumers, their critics now say, were too eager to buy big, expensive houses and fill them with the latest electronic gadgets.... The questions is, How do consumers learn how to deal with their finances? How do they learn how to invest and manage their money?

While some life skills, like learning to drive or how to roast a chicken, seem pretty straightforward, a lot of people remain in the dark when it comes to managing their personal finances.

"Money remains the elephant in the room," says Manisha Thakor, a financial advisor. "Personal finance, like parenting, is something we are all expected to just pick up as we go along." This is true, she said, across the economic spectrum, with even the best-educated high-earning adults often financially illiterate.

Those eager to learn often face a tidal wave of information, Ms. Thakor said. "It's too much and they give up."

Leona West, founder and chief executive of an online company, acknowledged she learned about finances the hard way. "When you're in serious debt in your 20s you have to learn pretty quickly. Sink or swim. I won't go into specifics about my debt, but it was hefty—enough for it to still be affecting my life 10 years later. I dug out by educating myself, doing loads of work on my self-esteem and, most importantly, changing my relationship with money."

Richard Andrews, 62, a former financial journalist, said he learned the most useful lessons about handling money from his family.

"My parents weren't particularly sophisticated about finances, but all of us had small allowances beginning when we started school," he said. His father made him and his sister "compute how much money we would need for a year, using the Sears, Roebuck catalog to price clothing and adding in items like school lunches and bus fare. What I learned from the clothing allowance was that if you want to save money, you can.

"I have always thought of money as freedom," he said. "It seems to me that other people think of it as something else: power, status. The freedom for me is from having to work or to work the job you really want."

In a culture constantly bombarding consumers with advertising couples with peer pressure to buy the biggest, best and latest of everything, resisting these messages is crucial, Mr. Andrews added. "Be Jones instead of trying to keep up with him."

Sally Chiappa, a 30-year old administrative secretary, said she began handling her own money when she was 5, with her first bank account. Whatever funds she received in gifts, baby-sitting and pet-sitting jobs, went into savings.

"I knew that saving my money was something that I could do and that I enjoyed watching my balance grow," she said.

Ms. Chiappa said she remains financially conservative. "I spend no more money than I keep in the banks and don't use credit cards. I have had absolutely no debt for the last five years and my credit rating is also around 800, and I'm really proud of that."

111

Moms-to-Be Have Urge to Splurge
Lansing, Michigan State Journal February 25, 2008
By Marshall Loeb

If you are expecting a baby, you may find yourself spending more money than you have to. But relaxing the purse strings for some non-essentials, as long as it doesn't wreak havoc with paying bills, is important.

In her new book, "Expecting Money: The Essential Financial Plan for New and Growing Families," national credit and money management expert Erica Sandberg details that could be worth the expense.

Pregnancy splurges are perhaps the most likely to pry dollars from your bank account. They are born of a desire to feel beautiful during pregnancy. No less tempting than spending on the mother-to-be is the desire to splurge on your baby. "You time" splurges are perhaps the most overlooked category."

Debt Relief Can Cause Headaches of Its Own
New York *Times* February 9, 2008
By Jane Birnbaum

It wasn't supposed to work this way. Credit card companies have long seduced customers with "buy now, pay later," hoping they would pay at least the minimum amount month after month but never pay off their debts. Now, though, with the economy slowing and houses no longer easy sources of cash, a growing number of consumers cannot pay even the minimums.

In December 2007, revolving debt—an estimated 95 percent from credit cards—reached a record high of $943.5 billion. The annual growth rate of this debt increased steadily in 2007. The amount of debt that is delinquent—in which payments are late but the accounts still open—also appears to be on the rise. Charge-offs—accounts closed for nonpayment—also grew in 2007 and banks expect charge-offs to keep rising in 2008.

What can borrowers do to extricate themselves? If belt tightening suffices, one option is a debt management repayment plan in which interest rates, but not balances, are reduced. (Bankruptcy may be an alternative for those who can't seem to get out of their debt) "sweat box."

Then there is debt settlement, when a debtor and a creditor agree that payment of a negotiated, reduced balance will be payment in full. "Done correctly, it can absolutely help people," said Cyndi Geeredes, an associate professor at the University of Illinois laws school who also runs a consumer debt clinic.

The experts agree, however, that "buyer beware" is the best advice when considering debt settlement companies. A thousand companies (including online companies) exist nationwide, up from about 300 a couple of years ago.

You Are What You Spend
New York *Times* February 10, 2008
By W. Michael Cox and Richard Alm

With markets swinging wildly... and the word "recession" on everybody's lips, renewed attention is being given to the gap between the haves and have-nots in America. Most of the debate, however, is focused on the wrong measurement of financial well-being.

It's true that the share of national income going to the richest 20 percent of households rose from 43.6 percent in 1975 to 49.6 percent in 2006. Income statistics, however, don't tell the whole story of Americans' living standards. Looking at a far more direct measure of American families' economic status—household consumptions—indicates that the gap between rich and poor is far less than most assume, and that the abstract, income-based way in which we measure the so-called poverty rate no longer applies to our society.

The top fifth of American households earned an average of $149,963 a year in 2006. They spent $69,863 on food, clothing, shelter, utilities, transportation, health care, and other categories of consumption. The rest of their income went largely to taxes and savings.

The bottom fifth earned just $9,974, but spent nearly twice that—an average of $18,153 a year. How is that possible? Lower income families have access to various sources of spendable money that doesn't fall under taxable income. These sources include sales of homes and cars and securities that are not subject to capital gains taxes.

(Also) to understand why consumption is a better guideline of economic prosperity than income, it helps to consider how our lives have changed. Nearly all American families have refrigerators, stoves, color TVs, telephones and radios. Air-conditioners, cars, VCRs or DVD players, microwave ovens, washing machines, clothes dryers and cellphones have reached more than 80 percent of households.

Tying it All Together

What would it be like if we actually taught children about money at an early age? We teach them how to do math, how to read and write, and—hopefully—how to get along with friends and others. Why not teach them about saving and spending and how to value things while also valuing "things other than things."

With rare exceptions, it seems early education about money and savings and spending has been left to the parents. But even sex education is taught in most schools these days—to what degree is debatable. Of course, how we teach about money would be equally debatable. Who would put together the curricula? Whose values would be expressed? Perhaps we could create a curriculum similar to a mid-level economics class, based more on facts and theories.

And then, there's the media. What to do about the media? The advertisers are going after the kids and they're taking no prisoners. Remember when kids used to just watch Sesame Street on public TV—no commercials? Even the Saturday morning cartoons commercials were tame compared to today's standards.

I remember when my Dad used to tell me: "when I was a boy, we used to have 50 different games we could play with a tennis ball and the side of a house." "Yeah, right," I used to think. Now, I find myself thinking the same thing when I compare my childhood in the '60s and '70s to the youth of today. Five year olds demand $100 electronic toys and then break or tire of them within days or weeks.

We each can stop, take a breath, and calm ourselves in the sea of endless desire and consumption. Either we can try to satisfy all our desires in a rush and then burst or we can learn to spread out our desires and enjoy life forever.

Notes & Reflections

Part Three

*Exercises for Recovering Over-shoppers
& Overspenders*

Questions for Self-Exploration

1. Recall your earliest memory of shopping or spending? What did you get?

2. What was going on in your life at the time that may have been significant?

3. What did you think and feel when you first shopped or spent money?

4. Was there anything symbolic about what you bought?

5. Were there any negative or positive consequences from your action?

6. Did you develop a habit of buying or spending soon afterwards or later? If so, how long was it?

7. When you were a child, did you witness someone else who bought or spent frequently or lavishly? If so, who was it and what was bought?

8. What was going on in your life at the time that may have been significant?

9. What did you think and feel about this other person's action(s)?

10. Are you aware of any negative or positive consequences for that person or for you because of that person's action(s)?

11. Did you develop a habit of buying things or spending money soon afterwards or later? If so, how long was it?

12. What was going on in your life at this time that was significant?

13. When you were a child would you say you were more deprived or spoiled? Both? Please elaborate.

14. Were your parents or caretakers good money managers? Explain.

15. Did anybody teach you any lessons about money— directly or indirectly—when you were young? If so, what?

16. Did you feel like your family had as much money and things, less than, or more than your neighbors and others?

17. Were you brought up with certain values around money and things? If so, what? Did you agree with those values?

18. Are there particular kinds of things that you buy or spend money on? What are they and why do you buy these kinds of things? From stores, online, elsewhere?

19. Have you ever had anything stolen from you whether money or an object? If so, how did that make you feel?

20. Have you noticed that you began to buy more things, larger things, more expensive things, or more frequently over time?

21. Are you more prone to shopping or buying at a particular time of the day, week, and year? If so, when and why is that?

22. Are you more prone to shopping or buying when you are in a certain mood? Anxious? Angry? Lonely? Depressed? Manic? Bored?

23. Are you more prone to shopping or buying when a certain event or circumstance occurs? If so, explain.

24. Do you actually use or derive benefit what you buy? Explain.

25. Are you able to distinguish between your desire for what you've bought and your need for it? If so, explain.

26. Do you experience strong feelings or physical sensations right before, during, or right after you've bought something? If so, describe the sensations and when they occur.

27. Do you tend to be perfectionist and need control or order? If so, do you think this is a factor in why you shop or spend?

28. Do you recognize any other addictive or compulsive behaviors in your life? What are they and how do they relate to your shopping/spending?

29. Who knows about your over-shopping/overspenidng and to what extent?

30. What prevents you from telling certain persons or from elaborating to the ones you have told?

31. List all the benefits, financial and emotional, that you have gotten out of shopping/spending? Be honest with yourself.

32. List all the financial, emotional, legal, and employment-related that over-shopping/overspending has cost you. Be honest with yourself.

33. Do you want to stop over-shopping/overspending? Why and why not?

34. What are you prepared to do to support yourself in stopping and starting again?

35. What have you learned about yourself from these questions?

BUDGETING 101

CURRENT MONTHLY INCOME:

From Primary Job: _____
From Secondary Job(s): _____
From other sources (stocks, bonds, etc) _____
Other miscellaneous income: _____
CURRENT TOTAL MONTHLY INCOME: _____

CURRENT MONTHLY LIVING EXPENSES:

Housing: _____
Transportation: _____
Vehicle Fuel: _____
Health/other Insurances: _____
Food: _____
Phone: _____
Electric: _____
Heating/Cooling: _____
Miscellaneous Repairs: _____
Clothing: _____
Entertainment: _____
Student Loans: _____
Taxes: _____
Other: _____
Other: _____
CURRENT TOTAL MONTHLY EXPENSES: _____

MONTHLY DEBT: *Not incl. home, car, or student loans*

Credit Card #1: _____
Credit Card #2: _____
Credit Card #3: _____
Personal: _____
Other: _____
CURRENT TOTAL Credit Card DEBT: _____

What have you learned or noticed? How do you feel?

_____
_____

A NEW BUDGET

Is there anything you can increase, reduce or reprioritize?

NEW MONTHLY INCOME:

From Primary Job: _____
From Secondary Job(s): _____
From other sources (stocks, bonds, etc) _____
Other miscellaneous income: _____
NEW TOTAL MONTHLY INCOME: _____

NEW MONTHLY LIVING EXPENSES:

Housing: _____
Transportation: _____
Vehicle Fuel: _____
Health/other Insurances: _____
Food: _____
Phone: _____
Electric: _____
Heating/Cooling: _____
Miscellaneous Repairs: _____
Clothing: _____
Entertainment: _____
Student Loans: _____
Taxes: _____
Other: _____
NEW TOTAL MONTHLY EXPENSES: _____

MONTHLY DEBT: *Not incl. home, car, or student loans*

Credit Card #1: _____
Credit Card #2: _____
Credit Card #3: _____
Personal: _____
Other: _____
NEW TOTAL Credit Card DEBT: _____

What have you learned or noticed? How do you feel?

_____

_____

My List of Unfair Things

Acknowledge that, at times, you feel like a victim and feel it as fully as you need to. But also acknowledge that you cannot change the past and you cannot control the future. Acknowledge that, in some way, this is may be related to why you over-shop or overspend—to undo or make-up for the past and buffer future pain and disappointment. And you got hooked. Where do we go from here?

What if we surrendered the notion of fairness altogether? What if we learned to live life on life's terms and accept that sometimes things go well, sometimes better than we thought, and sometimes they don't go as we wish? We all have our grievances...and we collect plenty of evidence and agreement from others about how we've been harmed. But there are too many days when we'd rather be right than be happy. So much of the world falls into this trap.

When do we really get to enjoy life? Can we ever just attune to a place of wonder, surrender, letting go and living in the moment? And if so, why doesn't it seem to last? We need to be careful about *dwelling* our feelings of self-pity and our thoughts about life being unfair. Making a list of unfair things helps us by putting it out there in a concrete way to take a look at it. *The goal is not to dwell in the list but to name it feel it, and release it.* You may wish to burn or bury the list afterward or share it with someone.

Think of all those things you hate about your life or feel are unfair. Really run with it! Don't hold back or edit yourself out of guilt. We've all been told not to complain or whine. Let it rip! Your intention is to get it out so you can let it go. What's the worst that can happen? You'll either end up in tears of sadness or tears of laughter, or both!

My List of Unfair Things

1.
2.
3.
4.
5.
6.
7.
8.
9.
10.
11.
12.
13.
14.
15.
16.
17.
18.
19.
20.

My Lucky Gratitude List

No matter how bad you feel your life has been, there is another side of the coin. You are still alive. You may not view that as a good thing. But recovery requires us to begin thinking in a new way. In my years of personal recovery and in counseling hundreds of clients, the worst case scenario rarely happens. That's not to say people didn't lose things–they do–but most of the time things turned fine in the long run. Many come to be grateful for their bottoming out: it steered them toward help and toward a greater appreciation of basic gifts: freedom, family, friends, health, comforts, and opportunities.

We made a list of unfair things because we needed to bring that out to see what keeps us from feeling grateful, lucky. It's like the old joke: What's the difference between a pessimist and an optimist? An optimist thinks this is the best of all possible worlds. A pessimist knows that it is. Or another way of saying it: An optimist's creed is, gratefully, "It doesn't get any better than this." A pessimist's creed is, ungratefully, "It doesn't get any better than this."

Is the glass half-full or half-empty is a trick question. Why even look at the glass like that? If there's water in it, be thankful there's water in it. If it's empty, why not be grateful there's a glass there to catch the water from wherever it comes? We get to choose which list to focus on.

Think about any lucky breaks you've had in life. Think of things that could have been worse but they're not. It's time to put your thinking cap on. If you are having trouble, ask someone close to you to prod you in the right direction.

My Lucky/Gratitude List

1.

2.

3.

4.

5.

6.

7.

8.

9.

10.

11.

12.

13.

14.

15.

16.

17.

18.

19.

20.

My Dream Job

Work is a big part of our lives. If you're bored or stuck in your job, write a description of your dream job if money didn't matter, if age didn't matter. Really go for it! Was it something you dreamt about as a kid? What excites you about it? Think big!

_____
_____
_____
_____
_____
_____
_____
_____
_____
_____
_____
_____
_____
_____
_____

What has kept you from going for it? Is shopping/spending somehow an attempt to make up for the pain of not living your dream job or career? Is it working? What steps can you take to move closer to your dream job, even on a part-time basis? Can you taste some of the dream even as a hobby?

_____
_____
_____
_____
_____
_____
_____
_____

Journaling

Journaling is an important tool—especially for recovering persons. Journaling may include diary-like writings, poems, doodles or drawings, recording of dreams, and checklists. Journaling is a great way to voice or vent whatever you're going through. It also helps you look back more objectively and clearly and recognize important patterns over time.

Another way to journal is, more simply, writing short sentences to help you identify feelings. Five primary feelings are happy, sad, mad, afraid, and guilt/shame.

I feel angry when you don't appreciate me.
I feel hurt when you bring up the past
I feel sad when you don't pay attention to me
I feel afraid when we have trouble paying the bills on time
I feel happy when we have quality time and don't criticize

Practice Journal Page

_____

_____

_____

_____

_____

_____

_____

_____

_____

_____

_____

_____

_____

_____

_____

_____

_____

A Visit to a Homeless Shelter or Soup Kitchen

There was a recent article in O (Oprah) magazine about a therapeutic exercise being used with surprising success with anorexics and bulimics. In addition to other standard treatments, the anorexics and bulimics (and overeaters, too?) are required to volunteer at a homeless shelter or soup kitchen where food is served. They are required to help prepare and serve the food to those in need. Apparently, the experience has a profound impact on most and assists in the cognitive restructuring around the anorexics and bulimics adverse relationship with food. They begin to value food and recognize that either denying food or bingeing and purging is, frankly, crazy.

In my own life, I've noticed when I've felt ungrateful about my station in life, volunteering at homeless shelters or soup kitchens put things into perspective. In my work with recovering shoplifters, I sometimes recommend they do the same when persistent feelings of "life is unfair" surface.

While I haven't tried this exercise with my clients who are compulsive shoppers or spenders, I have a feeling it may have an impact as well. Maybe bringing your kids will help them value money and thing. Try it and journal a bit about it.

_____

_____

_____

_____

_____

_____

_____

_____

_____

_____

_____

Gray Area Behaviors

All recovering people are prone to slip back into rationalization, intellectualization, minimizing, and plain denial. One of the most common ways we do this is by experimenting with "gray area behaviors." Gray area behaviors often seem like "lesser" forms of our primary addiction; however, they still compromise one's recovery and constitute a relapse.

For example, a recovering alcoholic whose primary drink was hard liquor might rationalize drinking beer, though it's obvious to others it's basically the same thing. The alcoholic may have agreed drinking beer was not acceptable but as his life became more manageable, he decided he could drink on occasion—a sip of champagne at wedding for instance.

Here are some other examples:

--The gambling addict no longer goes to the casinos but still bets on sports or buys lottery tickets
--The drug addict no longer uses heroin but still takes Tylenol with codeine
--The shoplifting addict no longer steals merchandise outright but begins to switch price tags or does false returns

Recovery from compulsive shopping or spending—like recovery from eating disorders or sexual addictions—can be a bit complex and confusing at times. Realistically, the goal is healthy shopping and healthy spending rather than total abstinence from shopping or spending. The typical goal for alcoholics, drug addicts, gambling addicts, and shoplifting addicts, however, is total abstinence.

Each of us draws our own "line in the sand" about what recovery means and what degree of addictive behavior we are willing to eliminate. Ongoing counseling and/or support groups help us explore, identify, and challenge these gray area behaviors. Deeper levels of understanding develop, and behaviors naturally change for the better.

The challenge for recovering shopaholics or spendaholics is that the goal is not total abstinence as it typically is for alcoholic, drug addicts, gamblers, and shoplifters. Recovery from compulsive shopping or spending is more akin to recovery from an eating disorder or a sexual addiction.

Recovery is about progress not perfection. It is an ongoing journey. But we never condone gray area behaviors; rather, we emphasize the costs: guilt and anxiety over, loss of faith, full relapse, humiliation, rejection when caught.

Your List of Gray Area Behaviors

List all your gray area shopping or spending behaviors. Be honest with yourself if with nobody else. Write down your rationalizations for engaging in these behaviors. You may also wish to write down your rationalizations as well as the negative costs or potential consequences of each.

EXAMPE

Gray Area Behavior

I. Treating myself or others to *big* gifts only on special occasions such as birthdays and holidays

Rationalizations

1. I'm not shopping or spending as much as I used to
2. Everybody buys gifts on such occasions
3. I'm working hard in recovery and deserve the reward
4. I'm buying more useful, valuable, durable gifts, not junk
5. Somebody bought me a nice gift and I have to return the favor by buying something at least as nice

Costs/Consequences

1. I am still in debt and buying these things is still stressful and keeping me in debt longer; I also reneged on my promise not to buy big things for a while
2. Everybody isn't a compulsive shopper or spender like me. Not everybody is in debt or recovery. What other people choose to do is not my concern—what I do is
3. There are other ways to reward myself besides shopping or spending and not as lavishly
4. I'm still spending money I don't have and putting too much focus on things
5. I can just thank him and know he probably don't expect me to get them something equally as expensive or I could politely explain my financial circumstances if need be

Gray Area Behavior
II. I got it on sale!

Rationalizations

1. I usually paid full-price for my purchases—that's progress
2. I would have needed to buy the item eventually why wait?
3. I'm working hard in recovery and deserve a little reward
4. I'm giving it to someone else—it's not for me
5. The item was going out of stock—this was my last chance

Costs/Consequences

1. I am still in debt and buying these things is still stressful and keeping me in debt longer; I also reneged on my promise not to buy big things for a while
2. I should wait till I'm out of debt and really needed it
3. There are other ways to reward myself besides shopping
4. I'm still spending money I don't have; I could give a card or create or recycle a gift
5. I wouldn't have died without it, nothing's that important

Your List of Gray Area Behaviors

1. _____
Rationalizations:

Costs/Consequences:

2. _____
Rationalizations:

Costs/Consequences:

3. _____
Rationalizations:

Costs/Consequences:

4. _____
Rationalizations:

Costs/Consequences:

5. _____
Rationalizations:

Costs/Consequences:

Better Ways to Get Freebies & Good Deals

We all love a bargain. We all love to get something for nothing. If you are a bargain shopper, you will need to be especially careful with this exercise. For others, this may be a valuable way of helping you save money on *occasional* purchases. Be creative and come up with some safe, fun, natural alternatives to fill that need *occasionally*. Note: if this exercise feels like a gray area behavior to you, don't engage.

Examples:

1. Coupons
2. Flea Markets/Thrift Stores
3. Only buy sale items
4. Go to free sample days
5. Create art or functional items through creativity
6. Festivals, art/health fairs often offer free stuff
7. Garage sales
8. Estate sales
9. Volunteer for experiment studies
10. Auctions

Others:

I credit Terence Gorski for following work on Triggers, Warning Signs and the exercise "How My Addiction Served Me." I also thank Personalized Nursing LIGHT House, Inc., for having employed me as a counselor to teach this material to hundreds of clients between 1997-2004. I have continued to use this material with my clients since then.

Common Triggers & Ways to Cope

Triggers are stimuli I encounter in my external environment, namely, people, places, things, or events—that can set off a chain reaction of thoughts and feelings leading to a relapse of over-shopping or overspending. A big part of recovery includes practicing avoiding triggers which put me at risk while also developing coping skills to deal with them if/when I need to. This will require lifestyle changes. *Some examples of triggers and coping skills may include:*

I. People

A parent, a friend, a co-worker, a sibling, (qualities may Include being critical, non-appreciative, abusive, neglectful or manipulative)

Coping skills:

1. Avoid, limit contact or length of time around
2. Have a heart-to-heart with about how I feel
3. Journal about my feelings
4. Talk about issues in support groups
5. Work on issues in therapy
6. Talk to family/friends about my feelings
7. Use self-talk/affirmations while visiting
8. Do deep breathing as feelings come up & leave
9. Write an e-mail or letter stating how I feel
10. Name my boundaries and behaviors I won't tolerate

II. Places

Stores, malls, garage sales, flea markets, restaurants, amusement parks, parties, or places where I may feel wrought with envy or jealousy

Coping skills:

1. Avoid or limit trips to stores, malls or other places
2. If I'm somewhere I'm feeling uncomfortable, I can leave or step outside to get centered
3. Find new places to spend time (gym, movies, museums, the park, my own home)
4. Attend support group meetings
5. Create a buddy system with positive people I look forward to spending time with
6. Take up a hobby
7. Do volunteer work
6. Go back to school or community college
7. Take life enhancement/personal growth courses
8. Get more invested in work at the office
9. Plant a garden or do yard work
10. Learn yoga or meditation

III. Things

Computers TV, clothing, catalogues, payday, credit cards and applications, advertisements, coupons

Coping skills:

1. Avoid or limit contact with triggering items
2. Cancel credit cards—or switch to debit cards
3. Cancel newspaper, magazine, catalogue subscriptions

4. Install pop-up blocker/website lock on websites
5. Self-talk: remind self that possessing the object will not bring happiness
6. Journal about my feelings/experience
7. Talk about feelings at in therapy or at a support group
8. Install TV channel blocks
9. Clean out house and begin a healthy creative project
10. Yell or exercise to burn off any tension created

IV. Events

Birthdays, holidays, parties, weddings, anniversaries, vacations, social engagements, entertainment events

Coping skills:

1. Increase my awareness that an event could bring up strong emotions and potential relapse (mark calendars)
2. Avoid or limit time at an event
3. Discuss feelings with a therapist or at a support group
4. Have a buddy stick near you to help support me
5. Journal my feelings
6. Pray and meditate
7. Make a balanced budget and stick to it
8. Don't isolate, hang out with good friends
9. Work out at health club, take sauna, hot tub
10. Remember the spirit or the intention of the holiday:
   It's not about the things, it's about connecting!

Common Warning Signs & Ways to Cope

Warning signs are stimuli in my internal environment (thoughts, feelings) as well as behavior patterns (lying, for example) which are like red flags. If unchecked, they build-up and will contribute to a relapse of over-shopping or overspending.

I. Thoughts

"I'm not appreciated," "I deserve a treat," "There's a sale"

Coping skills:

1. First, just begin to notice and identify the thought patterns
2. Counter this thought with a new thought such as "Thank you for sharing"
3. Do some deep breathing
4. Slow down, lie down or meditate on a new thought, my breath, or my body
5. Journal my thoughts and feelings
6. Talk to someone
7. Engage in primal scream or go for a walk to release stress
8. Pray to see things differently
9. Review or make a new gratitude list
10. Do volunteer work to help those less fortunate

II. Feelings

1. Anger, Anxiety, Disappointment, Loneliness, Boredom

Coping skills:

1. Notice the feeling pattern, don't judge it, don't give into it
2. Counter this feeling with self-talk: "Yes, I'm lonely right now but over-shopping or overspending doesn't help"

3. Begin deep breathing
4. Snap a rubber band around your wrist
5. Engage in primal scream or anger release like breaking a stick or hitting a pillow
6. Talk to a therapist, friend, or co-worker
7. Exercise
8. Journal feelings
9. Take yourself out on a date/read a book, watch a movie
10. Get a pet or play with the one(s) you have

III. Behaviors

Isolating, beginning to engage in "gray area" dishonesty, becoming passive and stuffing anger instead of asserting myself, judging others, stopping going to meetings, care taking others, stopping balancing my budget, lying

Coping skills:

1. Notice the behavioral pattern, acknowledge its danger
2. Begin deep breathing
3. Ask yourself why you are doing this; are you really committed to your recovery?
4. Speak with a therapist, friend, or sponsor
5. Journal about it
6. Go to a movie
7. Create something artistic
8. Go for a long walk
9. Pray or meditate
10. Clean, organize, or engage self in a project

List your top 10 triggers & coping skills:

Triggers	Coping Skills
1.	
2.	
3.	
4.	
5.	
6.	
7.	
8.	
9.	
10.	

List your top 10 warning signs & coping skills:

Warning Signs	Coping Skills
1.	
2.	
3.	
4.	
5.	
6.	
7.	
8.	
9.	
10.	

How My Addiction Served Me

Be honest. You know you were getting something out of your addiction. Despite the negative consequences, despite the attempts to stop and the powerlessness to do so, all addictions serve the addict. There is a payoff, a perceived benefit. It is crucial to get clear on this not only to increase your self-knowledge but to better implement ways to meet the needs you were trying to fill by stealing.

A key to recovery is developing new ways to cope with issues and new ways to get needs met. This takes patience and discipline. We get used to quick fixes to needs and develop robotic and automatic ways of satisfying ourselves.

For Example:

1. *I shopped or spent to calm my anger or to vent it out*

*<u>Payoff</u>: It protected me from my anger because I was afraid to feel it or release it more directly on others

*<u>Cost:</u> By shopping/spending as a way to suppress or express my anger, I now realize it didn't resolve my anger and made others angry at me which, in turn, made me angry at them and, eventually, at myself

*<u>New way to serve need.</u> I can work on my anger and my rage from past unresolved issues as well as when anger comes up in the present in therapy, in support groups; I can journal or exercise.

2. *I shopped or spent to fill the void of loss*

*<u>Payoff:</u> It helped distract me from the pain of the loss. It made me feel full for a while, complete. It numbed the pain. It filled the hole. It numbed the sadness, the anger

*<u>Cost:</u> By shopping or spending to fill the void of many losses in my life I realize I didn't allow myself to go through the necessary grieving process we all have to go through.

Through over-shopping and overspending, I lost much more.

*New way to serve need: I can attend support groups or counseling, create meaningful rituals (go to grave side, light a candle, focus on the good memories).

3. I shopped or spent to feel power, to feel control

*Payoff: I could get something (a thing or an experience) by buying it or spending money. It made me feel special and powerful. If I didn't have enough of something in my life— love, health, respect—shopping or spending made me feel less vulnerable for a while.

*Cost: I had an illusion of power and control but, eventually, the tables turned and I felt more disempowered and out of control. It became clear to me that my very inability to stop shopping and spending was a sign I had become a slave to it.

*New way to serve need: I will follow through with positive goals in my life and chart my success. I will remind myself that true power comes from with—from my strength of character—and from without—through my Higher Power. I will associate with people who help empower me and remind me of my strengths when I am down.

Exercise: Complete the following payoffs, costs, and new ways to serve your needs for the following ways you identify shopping and spending served you.

4. I shopped or spent to lift my-esteem when I felt inadequate

*Payoff:

*Cost:

*New way to serve need

145

5. *I shopped or spent to get a lift when I felt depressed*
*Payoff:

*Cost:

*New way to serve need:

---

6. *I shopped or spent to occupy myself when I was lonely*
*Payoff:

*Cost:

*New way to serve need:

---

7. *I shopped or spent to make life right when it seemed unfair*
*Payoff:

*Cost:

*New way to serve need:

---

8. *I shopped or spent to as a reward/entitlement for giving*
*Payoff:

*Cost:

*New way to serve need:

---

9. *I shopped or spent when afraid or anxious about things*
*Payoff:

*Cost:

*New way to serve need:

X. *I shopped or spent on self & others to make others like me*
*Payoff:

*Cost:

*New way to serve need:

Honesty Is Its Own Reward

"Honesty is its own reward" is an old saying and many of us were brought up believing this. Then something went awry. If honesty was so great, how come there were lies and secrets? The good guys didn't always finish first. At some point most of us learn not to be so naive about life. We learn things aren't always one or two dimensional. Rules, laws, commandments, and guidelines are meant to give us some direction and assistance. But giving up on honesty is a dangerous decision.

If you think about it: lying about finances or about purchases, or hiding accounts or items bought is akin to committing adultery: it's a betrayal. Trust is the bedrock of healthy relationships. And trust is shaken or broken where there is addiction.

Honesty is a quality often given lip service. But the children are watching, and listening, and learning. We need to take honesty seriously. If we want to be treated with honesty, we need to practice it. Honesty works. Honesty is its own reward.

Honesty promotes:

*Trust
*Self-esteem
*Being given responsibilities
*Good relationships
*Admiration and respect
*Spiritual connectedness, serenity
*Others being honest with you

Losing Your Edge or Gaining Your Edge?

Have you ever thought if you stopped shopping or spending you'd cease to exist? Do you think if you stopped shopping or spending, you'd "lose your edge"? What if you didn't have the latest gadget, or you stopped treating everyone to gifts or dinners, or you had to live low-key for a while? Would life really be that boring? Would you really be that boring?

What if the real edge is learning how to be ourselves? The real edge is having nowhere to run to when feeling angry, depressed or anxious. The real edge is surrendering control over our need for control, over our manipulating life from moment to moment—learning how to be where we need to be—right here, right now.

A person in true recovery is much more real than she was in her addiction. Her edge is more in full view now—whereas it used to be "behind the scenes" or "a front." Our edge is in our ability to be present, vulnerable, and authentic.

Still, we may need to grieve our loss of "slickness" and hyperactivity which we embodied during our days of shopping and spending. Hopefully, we'll actually learn to be grateful for what our addictive experience has taught us. Perhaps we'll appreciate the contrast between the busyness and the drama and the fluidity and the natural highs.

As we bring our new edge into life and into our relationships, we may feel uncomfortable and others may have to adjust to our new, emerging selves. But it will be worth it. There's no greater feeling than waking up excited to face the day and being able to lay one's head on the pillow at day's end knowing we caused no harm, we did the best we could and, maybe, we contributed just a little to life's solutions rather than its problems.

Be Assertive!

I am convinced most people over-shop or overspend because they're either not getting what they really want from life—love, attention, recognition, appreciation, security, purpose or passion—or because they're overwhelmed and overburdened by life or people for lack of setting good boundaries. Most of us have been trained not to be selfish, to put our needs last. We are not taught how to speak up for what we want and need. We are not taught to be assertive. We remain passive, become violent or aggressive, or act out passive-aggressively—including through shopping or spending. We may use shopping or spending as a weapon to get back at someone. One of the most common goals in recovery is how to be more assertive in our relationships--with spouses, family, children, friends, the boss, co-workers, everybody. Likewise, one of the most common reasons for relapse is lack of assertiveness which leads to a build-up of resentment and stress. There are many good books on how to be more assertive. Find one that works for you.

Have you asserted yourself lately? With whom and on what issue do you need to be assertive? When will you do it?

WHO?   WHAT ISSUE?   WHEN?

1. _____

2. _____

3. _____

4. _____

5. _____

The Importance of Humor

Having a sense of humor about my life and life in general has been one of my biggest challenges. Most addicts have a great sense of humor yet are incredibly sensitive and often take too much in, let too much affect them. We take on the world's pain at an early age; we either care too much or care too little. This must change: a healthy balance must arise. There's hardly a place more in need of humor than at work.

Given the pain and injustice many of us feel, the hardest thing is to laugh at ourselves. How do we do that? First, we need to rule out whether clinical depression or a chemical imbalance is contributing to our doldrums; consider seeing a psychiatrist. Second, we may be blocking energy by holding onto the past and/or fearing the future; consider seeing a therapist or joining a support group. Third, we may need to look at our current environment—family, friends, co-workers; maybe we need to be around people who know how to have healthy fun; consider joining a club, taking up a hobby, or learning stand-up comedy. Seriously! Fourth, diet and lifestyle may also affect our mood, energy, and outlook.

Laughter and joy live in the present moment. If you've ever caught yourself in a good belly laugh, you'll recall that you let go of your attachment to the past and to future. You were in the moment. True comedy is an art and a gift. It gives us back the gift of the present.

So what's so funny about being a shopaholic or spendaholic? Not much if you are in the throes of it. But can you at least see the absurdity of believing your peace and salvation comes from spending money or having things? It is sad to admit but true. You are not alone. Have you ever thought someone else's behaviors were ridiculous or childish? It's time to turn the mirror on ourselves! *The truth will set us free. But first it might piss us off.*

Many of us use humor as a defense mechanism or cover-up to protect ourselves from pain. We may receive benefits through humor unless our pain can no longer remain concealed. "Fake it till you make it" is a popular saying. This can work for a while.

Are you a recovering "serious person"? For those of us who grew up early and took on being reliable, responsible and self-sacrificing, the anger and pain takes a while to melt and give way to lightness, spontaneity and joy. Others before us have been able to realize this. What do you think prevents us from experiencing this? It is most likely, our own ego and stubbornness. This is recovery: letting go of the belief that life is unfair, cruel, unsafe, and empty.

"Let go and let God" is a favorite saying in recovery circles. But what does it mean? And how do you do it? When things aren't working out the way we'd like them to, we have choices: we can get angry or upset, we can give up and quit, or we can keep moving forward.

Can you laugh at yourself even in your most painful moments? Can you access a feeling of gratitude for what your addiction experience has taught you? Can you take your lemons from life and make lemonade?

How do you find humor? What makes you laugh? Schedule some time or activities for humor and laughter.

1. _____
2. _____
3. _____
4. _____
5. _____
6. _____
7. _____
8. _____
9. _____
10. _____

Someone to Talk to

All addictions thrive on shame and secrecy. It's imperative you find at least one trustworthy person you can share your story with. Some people in your life already know or have some idea you have a problem with shopping or spending. *We're only as sick as our secrets.*

Hopefully, you confide in someone with the intention of getting support to help stop a behavior; if not, a "confession" just to get something off your chest is a start. It's not the listener's job to fix or save you. The listener may ask: do you just want me to listen or do you want some advice? If the listener isn't sure what advice to give, a good fallback is always: "I encourage you to seek professional help."

If the listener is a loved one, he or she may choose to say something like: "I'm glad you have shared this secret with me. I appreciate your trust in me. You are not a bad person but this behavior is destructive to you, to others (and to us). I need you to commit to getting help for this immediately because our relationship cannot be healthy as long as you are doing this and I can't be in a relationship like this."

Recovery is an ongoing and deepening commitment to changing behavior patterns which, in turn, change you. Stopping over-shopping and overspending is a process which, over time, results in a stronger ability to choose and commit to life. Each day we must make a choice whether or not to shop or spend and to what degree. Some days this is not a big deal; on others, it is extremely hard to resist returning to the old ways of trying to cope with feelings and life.

But the bottom line is this: over-shopping and overspending do not help me. They don't solve anything and never will. As they say in recovery: "Once is too many times and a thousand times is never enough."

What to Do with Your Useless Purchases

For people who over-shop or overspend, clutter and hoarding often go hand-in-hand. Those I've counseled often struggle with parting with the things they've bought. This can be a difficult decision. *There's something primal about possession.*

But letting go of our attachment to what was bought can be valuable and powerful. It is not only about letting go of the object but, also, letting go of what the object has represented. Would you really die or disappear without any object? Holding onto things is, often, holding onto the past. We want to move forward. No pain, no gain. It is also a part of a making of amends as, typically, a spouse or other family member will appreciate the uncluttered space and be encouraged by the symbolic act of the new, emerging you.

But timing and pacing are both key. There's a line between letting go too abruptly and dragging your feet. When you feel ready to let go of the any goods, I suggest you do so a little at a time, throwing them away, donating them, or safely returning them to the store. Maybe you can have a garage or lawn sale. Are there any things that can be tastefully recycled as gifts? If you have a therapist, please work with him or her on this process. Have someone to whom to be accountable.

My List of Things to Let Go of
1.
2.
3.
4.
5.
6.
7.
8.
9.
10.

The Dangers of Transferring Addictions

When recovering addicts interrupt an addiction, they have a tendency to return to earlier addictions, develop new addictions, or cross to addictions "already in progress." Example: an ex-smoker begins overeating; a recovering alcoholic begins slamming the caffeine. Recovering addicts also often wind up in dysfunctional relationships early in recovery. Here are some common addictions which recovering shopaholics or spendaholics need to beware of.

Overeating/Bulimia

With all the stories about mounting debt, people continue to shop and spend like there's no tomorrow. Similarly, with all the stories about rising obesity rates, overeating continues to increase. It is one of the quickest, easiest, and, often, least expensive ways to reward or numb ourselves. Many people "emotionally eat" when experiencing strong or uncomfortable emotions—they literally eat their feelings to keep them down. Similarly, bulimic bingeing and purging is akin to shopping and returning. The consequences can be deadly. Please seek out a nutritionist and/or eating disorders specialist immediately. O.A. (Overeaters Anonymous) groups may also be helpful.

Gambling Addiction

For those who miss the thrill and excitement of shopping or spending or who are prone to live on the edge, gambling—especially casino gambling—can be a vicious trap. The casinos can easily remind one of stores. Both are beautiful public places with people milling around. The employees are nice to you. Lights flash and music may be playing. You are handing over money for something—in the case of gambling, the chance to win more money. For bargain shoppers, gambling may seem like a chance to get something for relatively little. But the consequences are high. As we did with over-shopping or overspending, we likely will gamble away our money, our time, our freedom, our relationships, our self-dignity, and our future. Gambling addiction, incidentally, has the highest rate of suicide of all addictions. Please seek out a gambling addiction specialist immediately. G.A. (Gamblers Anonymous) groups may also be helpful

Shoplifting/Employee Theft

A lot of people who shoplift or steal from work often are already shopaholics or overspenders as we've seen in some of the stories in this book. It is tempting to start shoplifting or stealing from work to help reduce debts or to save money with which to shop or spend. Shopaholics may find themselves still going to stores and may feel conflicted about spending and, so, may shoplift. Anger or other dissatisfaction at home may be mirrored or acted out in the workplace through embezzlement. Entitlement is a key motivation for those who steal and over-shop. Bargain shoppers, especially, may be driven to get something for nothing. The consequences of stealing can be devastating legally, financially and relationally. Please seek out a theft disorders specialist immediately. C.A.S.A. (Cleptomaniacs And Shoplifters Anonymous) groups may also be helpful.

Co-Dependency

When the illusion of who you think you are begins to dissolve with the letting go of over-shopping or overspending, one often feels lost for a while as he or she begins to reclaim or create a new self. It can be scary. There's a loss of ritual, loss of image, loss of things, and a void. Naturally, it's quite common for one to seek out others to live through—either others who have problems or others who seem on top of the world. Beware of trying to find yourself through another. Seek out a skilled counselor and Alanon or CODA meetings.

Forgiving Ourselves

It's hard forgiving others who have harmed us. It's hard forgiving life, God, the world, for not living up to our hopes and expectations. Forgiving ourselves, however, may be the hardest journey of all.

Are you self-critical? Is there a tape always playing inside your head? Is it hard to forgive yourself for things you did in the past? How do you think it would feel to no longer be holding onto any guilt or shame over hurting anyone in your life—including yourself? How long will you hold on? This may be the only life we have to live. If God can forgive—as many believe—how arrogant is it of us not to do so? How hypocritical is it of us to counsel others to forgive but not do so? Can we forgive ourselves and others just for being human? After all, being human means "capable of mistakes."

"Shame" stands for:

SHOULD
HAVE
ALREADY
MASTERED
EVERYTHING

I forgive myself for _____

I forgive myself for _____

I forgive myself for _____

I forgive myself for _____

I forgive myself for _____

I forgive myself for over-shopping/overspending.

I forgive myself. I forgive myself. I forgive myself.

What do you need to forgive yourself for?

12 Steps of Alcoholics Anonymous

1. We admitted we were powerless over alcohol — that our lives had become unmanageable.

2. Came to believe that a Power greater than ourselves could restore us to sanity.

3. Made a decision to turn our will and our lives over to the care of God as we understood Him.

4. Made a searching and fearless moral inventory of ourselves.

5. Admitted to God, to ourselves and to another human being the exact nature of our wrongs.

6. Were entirely ready to have God remove all these defects of character.

7. Humbly asked Him to remove our shortcomings.

8. Made a list of all persons we had harmed, and became willing to make amends to them all.

9. Made direct amends to such people wherever possible, except when to do so would injure them or others.

10. Continued to take personal inventory and when we were wrong promptly admitted it.

11. Sought through prayer and meditation to improve our conscious contact with God, as we understood Him, praying only for knowledge of His will for us and the power to carry that out.

12. Having had a spiritual awakening as the result of these steps, we tried to carry this message to alcoholics, and to practice these principles in all our affairs.

12 Steps of Debtors Anonymous

1. We admitted we were powerless over debt—that our lives had become unmanageable.

2. Came to believe that a Power greater than ourselves could restore us to sanity.

3. Made a decision to turn our will and our lives over to the care of God as we understood Him.

4. Made a searching and fearless moral inventory of ourselves.

5. Admitted to God, to ourselves, and to another human being the exact nature of our wrongs.

6. Were entirely ready to have God remove all these defects of character.

7. Humbly asked Him to remove our shortcomings.

8. Made a list of all persons we had harmed and became willing to make amends to them all.

9. Made direct amends to such people wherever possible, except when to do so would injure them or others.

10. Continued to take personal inventory and when we were wrong promptly admitted it.

11. Sought through prayer and meditation to improve our conscious contact with God as we understood Him, praying only for knowledge of His will for us and the power to carry that out.

12. Having had a spiritual awakening as the result of these steps, we tried to carry this message to compulsive debtors, and to practice these principles in all our affairs.

Copyright © A.A. World Services, Inc. Adapted and reprinted with permission.

It may be helpful to contemplate one step at a time and write down some thoughts and feelings that come up for each step.

Step One

Admitted we were powerless over our debt (shopping and spending)—that our lives have become unmanageable.

"Denial is not just a river in Egypt" is a popular saying in recovery circles. We may tell ourselves: "my behavior is a choice. I can stop anytime." There may, indeed, be periods of time where we are able to stop. This is very common.

Ultimately, however, we are powerless if we always feel compelled to come back the problematic behavior. Powerlessness is akin to "not getting the lesson."

Manageability is another concept where we can be in denial. We may have a high tolerance for chaos and disorder whereas others around us see pure unmanageability. If we have a hunch we're having trouble with money, grades, romance, emotions, or clarity of purpose—that's a pretty good sign things have become unmanageable. The only question is how long with our unmanageable lives become so bad that something truly devastating occurs.

WAKE UP!

It's time to admit shopping or spending has taken over our lives! It has taken over! Our lives have become unmanageable. Shopping or spending can't help—they hurt us... and others. We've lived a life of lies, of smoke and mirrors. If shopping or spending were the solution, why are we still depressed, anxious, unhappy, unfulfilled? What problems have multiplied?—legal, financial, work, health, self-esteem, relationships, spiritual? For many of us, it was all of the above. But there is hope.

Powerless is how we felt at some earlier point in our lives and we tried to get our power back through shopping or spending. But it didn't work. We eventually felt even more powerless over our lives and, in addition, over our shopping or spending. We need to return to the sanity of Step 1.

_____

_____

_____

_____

_____

_____

_____

_____

_____

_____

Step Two

Came to believe that a Power greater than ourselves could restore us to sanity.

It's often said in recovery circles: do not make another person our Higher Power. For a short time, we may need to. This Higher Power can be a therapist, a minister, a sponsor, a financial advisor, anyone whose guidance seems to be wiser than our own. Our Higher Power may be a support group. Eventually, we must tap into the source of universal truth, wisdom and sanity.

In our asking for help we must have an inherent belief that we could also be restored to sanity—even if we've never known sanity. Many of us don't know how to define sanity, much less experience it. On some level, we know our lives have become insane and would just get worse without help. Perhaps we need to view sanity as a continuum.

What does sanity mean to you? Is sanity a world where money and things rule? Or does it mean thinking and behaving in a way that really works? Does it mean neither running from nor being overwhelmed by our feelings? Does it mean living not in the past or the future, but in the present as much as possible? Is it a state of inner peace and knowing that no matter what happens everything will work out?

Over-shopping and overspending are outward insane expressions of our inner insanity and angry, fearful, twisted thinking. There are those who view life as insane and have rationalized that shopping or spending were sane behaviors in an insane world. Many of us believe our addictions are a logical and sane response to life.

In time, we become more spiritual and can access our Higher Power. To do this, we stop or slow down and breathe. We ask ourselves the right questions and allow ourselves to be guided by the Higher Power and wisdom within ourselves.

_____

_____

_____

_____

_____

_____

_____

_____

_____

Step Three

Made a decision to turn our will and our lives over to the care of our Higher Power as we understood this.

It's one thing to admit we've got a problem and that our lives have become a wreck; it's another to admit that we need help and, in a moment of faith, believe that something better is possible for us. But it's a quantum leap to turn our will over, the way we've always known.

Step Three is the hardest step for many. It's so easy to go in and out of taking our will back—our old ways of thinking and doing things. Step Three challenges us to resist our will or desire to take shortcuts in life—or giving into all or wants just because we want it. Step Three also challenges us to surrender our attachment to how we think life should go. After all, this may be part of what prompted our shopping or spending to begin with: feeling life was unfair and we were entitled to make up for it.

When faced with the temptation to over-shop or overspend the "lower power" in us would have us believe there is no other way to ease the pain—we are entitled to do so and not to do so is actually a defeat rather than a victory. The ego is that part of us that speaks first and speaks loudest. When asked what we want, this part of us says: "I want that thing. I want to hurt someone. I want to get even. I deserve this!" Our Higher responds, when I surrender, to what I *really* want: peace, love, cooperation, a sense of meaning.

Step Three asks us to turn our lives over to the care of our Higher Power. We've probably said: "I've trusted before and look what happened? My way may not be the best way but if it doesn't turn out, at least I can blame myself." Step Three requires a leap of faith. If nothing changes, nothing changes.

It's no wonder most of us, especially addicts, have trouble letting go of our own way and being open another. When we do this for moments at a time, things usually turn out better than if we had tried to manipulate or handle it ourselves. Our Higher Power can even guide us to the help of others and to help others, too.

Step Four

Made a searching and fearless moral inventory of ourselves.

Step Four challenges us to stop blaming the world and others and to look at ourselves. This may feel difficult to do when we fall back into feeling like victims. In Step Four we look within—not only at our shopping or spending—at all our less honorable behaviors. We confront our shadow side, the things we don't want to claim, and the aspects of ourselves we may project onto others.

In working Step Four we also need to *recover* the positive aspects of ourselves—the moral parts of ourselves—which, due to our shame, we had lost touch with. We have to recover those parts of us such as the truly caring, honest, wonderful parts. In some ways, it may be more difficult for us acknowledge the positive aspects of ourselves than to acknowledge the negative ones.

_____

_____

_____

_____

_____

_____

_____

_____

_____

_____

Step Five

Admitted to our Higher Power, to ourselves, and to at least one other human being, the exact nature of our wrongs.

Step Five challenges us to not just share the general details about our behavior but, also, the exact nature of our wrongs. That means how much and how long and any other details we've been lying about or not disclosing. The exact nature of our wrongs includes not just the details about our shopping and spending but our wrongful thinking underneath: our selfishness, our greed, our controlling.

Further, we must share not just the truth with ourselves or with our Higher Power, but also with at least one other human being to make it more real. It's like writing something down vs. just remembering it in our heads. It is advised to first choose someone who can listen calmly and without judgment or attachment—such as a minister, sponsor, support group member, or close friend.

_____

_____

_____

_____

_____

_____

_____

_____

_____

_____

Step Six

Were entirely ready to have our Higher Power remove our defects of character.

Step Six is a little like Step Three. Being entirely ready to do anything is scary for most; to open for real and deep change can feel like facing death, surrendering to death, leaping off a cliff into the great abyss.

What are meant by defects of character? Perhaps they are traits which lead us to cause suffering in ourselves or others. These traits can include impatience, perfectionism, greed, dishonesty, selfishness, etc. Step Six—as with all the Steps—is unlikely to be mastered but, rather, constantly practiced. We need not fear having to get it right the first time—that's our perfectionism. Yet, we want to challenge ourselves and not drag our feet either.

We move into Step Six when we have worked through the first five. We enter with a spirit of sincerity and purity in each moment. We meditate on it and open ourselves to the inner wisdom and power of it as best as we can. We can be curious. After a while, we won't need our character defect list in front of us—we know what they are.

_____

_____

_____

_____

_____

_____

_____

_____

_____

_____

Step Seven

Humbly asked our Higher Power to remove our shortcomings.

Shortcomings and character defects are related. An example of a character defect is impatience. A shortcoming may be how our impatience expresses itself in the world around us: in traffic, with our spouses, in long lines. Perfectionism is a character defect—criticizing others who don't share our standard of perfection is a shortcoming. Over time, we will gain increasing clarity what our shortcomings are.

Step Six emphasizes the word "humbly" because it reminds us we can't do it ourselves. We don't make demands on our Higher Power; we ask and we are patient. As addicts, we put our faith outside ourselves—in quick fixes—whether in drugs, gambling, or shopping or spending. Recovery wisdom recognizes each Step is an ongoing process. We may need to ask many times for our shortcomings to be removed or dissolved as we become more and more ready.

_____
_____
_____
_____
_____
_____
_____
_____
_____
_____

Step Eight

Made a list of all persons we have harmed and became willing to make amends to all.

Our secret, addictive lives deprived us of authentic and loving relationships with others and also an equal opportunity for others to have authentic and loving relationships with us.

Our list may include parents, significant others, siblings, children, friends, co-workers, and others. We spend time imagining the harm we've done to them. This may be difficult due to overwhelming guilt, because we may not see directly the damage our behavior has caused, or because we may slip back into feeling like we, ourselves, have been the real victims in our lives. Nevertheless, we make a list of those we've harmed and do our best to name the specific harm, be it financial, emotional or both.

_____
_____
_____
_____
_____
_____
_____
_____
_____
_____

Step Nine

Made direct amends wherever possible except when to do so would injure people.

Making direct amends is another ongoing process. Amends may begin with an apology but usually requires more. It is often said: *The best amend we can give to our friends, family and society is to develop a good recovery program and ceasing to engage in insane, destructive behavior.* Making amends for lost trust takes time and patience; respecting people and money each day is a great way to start.

Paying off debts and/or returning or selling goods purchased may also be necessary. When might our amends hurt others financially or emotionally? We need to carefully consider this and get feedback from others who may help. As those who have completed this step will attest—it really helps with forgiveness—from others and for ourselves.

_____

_____

_____

_____

_____

_____

_____

_____

_____

_____

Step Ten

Continue to take personal inventory and when we are wrong promptly admit it.

This step is very important as recovery is an ongoing process of unraveling and letting go of the past and reclaiming a better way of living. In the meantime, we are living in the present, creating new conflict or karma each day, each moment. If we clean up after ourselves as we go along, we have less mess to clean up later. Keep it simple. One of the biggest gifts we get out of recovery is the ease to admit when we're wrong. To admit "I was wrong," "you are right," or "I am sorry," is to experience liberation. Especially good times to take a personal inventory are at the end of the day, in a support group setting, or anytime something is bothering us.

_____
_____
_____
_____
_____
_____
_____
_____
_____
_____

Step Eleven

Sought through prayer and meditation to improve our conscious contact with our Higher Power as we understood this, praying only for knowledge of our Higher Power's will for us and the power to carry out that will

Some may ask: "why pray or meditate? I'm not over-shopping or overspending anymore, my life is manageable again." We addicts are good at fooling ourselves into thinking we have control again—we were the sole cause of the problem and the sole solution. This can seem like an empowering belief but it can be potentially dangerous. Our thinking may be our worst enemy or our best friend. Einstein said: "the problems of the world cannot be solved at the level of thinking when the problems were created."

Working an ongoing recovery program helps us think more clearly. Left to our own devices and without checks, accountability, and support, we likely will return to our old thinking. Prayer and mediation help foster new ways of thinking. There are many forms of prayer and meditation. They can help us connect to our whole self, our center, and bring forth our most authentic and powerful self. Without prayer and meditation, the ego often runs rampant.

_____
_____
_____
_____
_____
_____
_____
_____
_____
_____

Step Twelve

Having had a spiritual awakening as a result of these steps, we will try to carry this message to other addicts and practice these principles in all our affairs.

Step Twelve is not an end but a beginning. It is the logical turnaround before returning to Step One. "We only keep what we give away" is a common recovery saying. If we truly have achieved some level of spiritual awakening through our recovery, why would we want to keep it to ourselves? This is not a call to go out on the street corner and start preaching and recruiting. But we can carry recovery as a gift to share with others who may show up in our lives—whether at a meeting table as a newcomer or in our daily affairs. We may need to be careful about trying to save others when we are the primary ones we need to save. There's a balance. We shall find that balance one day, each day, readjusting from moment to moment. One day at a time.

_____

_____

_____

_____

_____

_____

_____

_____

_____

_____

The Twelve Steps of Alcohols Anonymous have been reprinted with the permission of Alcoholics Anonymous World Services, Inc ("AAWS"). Permission to reprint and adapt the Twelve Steps does not mean that Alcoholics Anonymous is affiliated with this program. A.A. is a program of recovery for alcoholism only—use of A.A.'s Steps or an adapted version of its Steps in conjunction with programs and activities which are patterned after A.A., but which address other problems, or use in any other non-A.A. context, does not imply otherwise.

171

The Serenity Prayer

God,
Grant me the serenity to accept the things I cannot change,
The courage to change the things I can,
And the wisdom to know the difference. (Just for today)

_____
_____
_____
_____
_____
_____
_____
_____
_____
_____
_____
_____

<u>Note:</u> There are few if any support group meetings called "Shopaholics Anonymous." I have had some clients who have attended Debtors Anonymous meetings and gotten good support while others have attended and have said they didn't feel like it was a good fit for them. Some of those clients had shopping problems but not necessarily debt problems; thus, they couldn't seem to relate. A few other clients shared how they felt self-conscious due to wide gulfs between socio-economic classes: some group members claimed smaller debts while others were monumental.

There are some "virtual" support groups online through www.yahoogroups.com for shopaholics or compulsive shoppers that might feel like a better fit. Or, you can start your own group.

Part Four

Related Issues

Conducting an Intervention

"Intervention is a process by which the harmful, progressive, and destructive effects of (an addiction) are interrupted and the (addict) is helped to stop (the addiction) and to develop new and healthier ways of coping with his or her needs or problems. (Or more simply) presenting reality to a person out of touch with it in a receivable way." Vernon Johnson, from Intervention

Interventions have been around a long time. They have also garnered more widespread attention in the public. For example, in early 2005, The Arts & Entertainment Cable TV Channel (A & E) began airing an hour-long weekly series called "Intervention." The program follows the lives of real people near the bottom of their various addictions and, unbeknownst to them, culminates in actual interventions with family, friends, and a trained interventionist. There's also A & E's "Big Spender" series which debuted in 2007 featuring interventionist Larry Winget confronting out-of-control shoppers and spenders. I urge people to watch either of these series to learn about addiction and intervention.

I've worked with family members and friends of addicts who've struggled with whether, how, or when to confront or intervene with a loved one. For family or friends of a loved one with a shopping or spending problem, this can be challenging because of the shame and misunderstanding about these behaviors and the few resources to direct them to for help. It's tempting to shout: "Hey, cut it out! Stop shopping! Stop spending so much!"—as if it was only that easy. This approach likely will only push the person farther away from opening up, getting help, and stopping the behavior.

I've talked to parents of children who over-shop or overspend or don't know how to save or who just want and want and want. *Two approaches don't work:* saying or doing nothing, which sends an unspoken message it is not a big deal; and shaming, yelling, condemning, which sends the indirect message "you are bad" and pushes a child into shutting down his or her feelings. Children need to learn healthy attitudes about money and things and good money and object management—so do adults.

Most people are unaware, at least for a long period of time, that a loved one has a problem with shopping, spending or debt. The person usually hides his or her problem or downplays it with explanations or plain lies. The "evidence" often is circumstantial—clothes or debt collection notices piling up—and you may hesitate to confront someone. But there's a difference between a confrontation and an intervention. One typically confronts in the early stages; intervention usually is necessary after the problem has been brought to the light but nothing seems to be improving.

If you are reading this book, you hopefully have some knowledge and sensitivity about the dynamics and reasons people over-shop or overspend. Remember, it's often an unconscious cry for help. It's easy to be mad at someone but he or she is in pain. You also have the advantage of pointing a person who needs help in the right direction: to this book, to our web site, to counseling, to support groups, or to the various resources listed at the back of this book.

Even the intervention process is a starting point of a longer care process. Once the person admits a problem, you must be firm with consequences if he or she fails to follow through with finding further help. Share options with your loved one and offer reasonable assistance. If the intervention does not work, you may need to try again or make some hard choices so you can take care of yourself. Ultimately, a person has to be ready for change. The intervention is designed to speed along that process.

James Prochaska and Carlo DiClemente, psychologists, developed a model to illustrate the five stages of change:

1) pre-contemplation
2) contemplation
3) investigation/preparation
4) implementation
5) maintenance

Where does a loved one fall in this model? How about you?

You need supportive people at an intervention who have observed firsthand any of the over-shopping or overspending behaviors, the circumstantial clues of the behaviors, or any other problems associated with the suspected or known behaviors (mood swings, evasiveness, and change of lifestyle or interests). If you are the only one who can be involved in the intervention, so be it, but I would suggest you invite at least one trusted mutual friend, minister, counselor or family member to attend. In intervention is best done in person though I've known of interventions which took place by phone or even live chat due to travel and location obstacles.

An intervention is not a debate, discussion, or argument. You ask the person to listen as you and others outline and express your concerns (often in writing and read out loud) based on what you've observed as well as a sincere request for the person to get help immediately. Some resources are already researched and available should the person be ready to accept them. Sometimes the person will sit and listen without interruption, sometimes they will walk out, and sometimes they will interrupt throughout.

Here is an example of an intervention. A bit of background:

"Bill" has arranged a time at home to get his wife "Carol's" undivided attention. He and Carol have had several heated discussions over the last few years about her shopping and spending. Carol would make some attempts to curtail her behavior for a while but she always seemed to start-up again. Bill has invited his wife's sister, "Barbara," over because she's also recognized her sister's pattern of shopping and spending for a long time and he needs her support.

Bill has recently found some clothes in a basement closet with the price tags still on them. Further, he has intercepted a piece of mail indicating a credit card statement from an unfamiliar company. He hesitated to open it out because it addressed to his wife—but his curiosity and paranoia got the better of him. He figured he could say he opened it by accident. In the envelope he discovered a bill for nearly $10,000—all discretionary expenditures, mostly for clothing.

Bill times the intervention when Carol comes home from work.

Bill: Honey, I'm glad you're here. Barbara and I have something important to talk to you about and all we ask is that you listen. We'll give you a chance to talk when we're done. We need you to listen because we care about you.

Carol: What's this all about?

Bill: We're here because we care about you. We're here to talk about you about something we see. We're not accusing but we believe you have a serious problem with shopping and spending money and we think you need professional help. We need you to listen to what we need to say.

Carol: Shopping and spending? What are you talking about?

Bill: We know you feel taken off-guard. But we need you to listen to our concerns. For the last two years we've been having discussions about this. Things haven't really changed—they've just gotten worse. Yesterday, I found half a closet of new clothes hanging in the cedar closet downstairs. I've never seen you wear a single item. Most of them had the price tags still on them.

Carol: What are you doing snooping around? What does this have to do with anything?

Bill: Let me finish. There's something else. Today when I got the mail, I accidentally opened up a bill. I didn't know what it was but, apparently, it's a charge account you opened that I had no idea about. There's almost $10,000 owed on it—mostly for clothing.

Carol: What are you doing opening up my mail? And what are you doing here Barbara?

Barbara: Carol, I care about you and I know there's something wrong. Something's going on with you. I've noticed in the last couple of years you've been spending more money on things—nice things—more gifts, just more stuff. We want to help. We did some research and found out a lot of people over-shop when they have stress or other issues. You've been through a lot lately and you remember some of the things you told me a while ago that have been bothering you.

Carol: I don't know what you two are talking about. You're making a mountain out of a molehill. Those clothes in the cedar closet are things I've gotten on sale and am thinking of taking back or donating if need be. As for *my* credit card bill you "accidentally" opened, I have it under control. It's none of your business. I have my own money and I'm entitled to spend what I want with it and pay off my bills in my own time. Don't worry. If I die you'll get the life insurance if you're worried about getting stuck with my bills!

Bill: Honey, don't even talk like that. Please listen. Over the last two years since your mother died you haven't been the same. You quit going to the gym. We agreed to tighten our budget to save more for retirement but you haven't reduced your spending at all. Neither one of us has gotten a raise in a while. I'm not criticizing you, I'm just very concerned.

Carol: I don't keep track of things like I used to! You used to complain that I was too tight with money—now I'm too loose with it? Make up your mind! I can't seem to do anything right! Not here, not at work! Nowhere! I buy people gifts and they complain! No wonder I'm spending money!

Bill: Honey, calm down. I'm just asking you to listen to our concerns. We care about you and know something is wrong.

Carol: Nothing's wrong except for you both accusing me.

Barbara: Carol, c'mon, it's me. Get real. Something's obviously going on or you wouldn't be so angry and defensive. We're trying to help you.

Carol: You always were the know-it-all, weren't you? Why are you meddling in this anyway? You're one to talk. You've got your own marriage problems!

Barbara: Carol, this is about you right now. We want to help you. You're my sister. You need to trust us. These secrets you've been keeping have got to be eating you up inside. We just want to see you get some help. I miss the old Carol.

Bill: We're not going to tell anybody else what's going on if that's what you're worried about. But we need you to tell the truth here and agree to get some help or there will be consequences.

Carol: Consequences? What consequences?

Bill: There have already been consequences: a loss of trust. Carol, if you don't get honest here and own up to what's going on I don't think our marriage can survive. I don't think you can survive. If you don't get help, I will. I'll go to a counselor myself and find out what I need to do. In the meantime, this spending and keeping things from me has got to stop! If you don't take this opportunity for help now, I won't be the one to bail you out.

Lori: You don't have to worry about me.

Bill: This is a sickness. I need you to tell me the truth. What is going on with you? What's with the clothes, the credit card bill? What else don't I know? Why are you doing this?

Barbara: Carol, I don't need any fancy gifts and neither do my kids. We want to have the real Carol back.

Carol: I'm not going to give you any fancy gifts! And I don't know if the real Carol's coming back. There is no real Carol! All I've ever done is give to all of you. I've given my life for you. Nobody appreciates what I've had to sacrifice. If Mom were here right now...

It is best to let the person vent for a bit if they need to.

Carol: (on the verge of tears) There's so much pressure. I just can't take it. I'm always last. I don't ask for anything. I have needs, too! Nobody ever seems to notice.

Bill: (resisting the urge to save her) It's okay, honey. That's why we're here. We can work on things together but only if I know what's really wrong. But first, we need you to admit—you've got a problem.

Carol: (after a long pause and a deep inhale) I've got a problem...

Barbara: And are you willing to stop and get help today?

Carol: What kind of help? What does that mean? I can't take any time off work.

Barbara: "Carol, we're not going to tell anybody anything right now. That should be up to you and a therapist. But you need to get help right now before things get worse. You can take a medical leave if need be, whatever, just do it. Do it for you. We have the name of a therapist who specializes in treating compulsive shopping and spending.

Carol: Do you think I'm... a shopaholic?

Bill: I don't know. Maybe you are. Somebody's going to help you figure it out so you can get help. You're going to get through this. You're going to be all right. We'll stand by you if you take that step.

Carol: I feel so ashamed. I don't know how this happened to me. I don't know how I got into this mess. I'm afraid. I guess I don't have a choice, huh?

Bill: No, you have a choice... and so do we. And we're not going to choose to just watch you ruin your life and ours. We can't be a part of that. That's our choice.

Barbara: You took a big step today sis. I love you. It's going to be all right.

Carol: Okay. I hear you. I'm just so afraid. I don't even know what I'm afraid of. I know I need help. Please forgive me. I don't know what came over me these last two years.

Bill and Barbara: You've got it. We're on your side. Now, let's follow through with that phone call.

Notes & Reflections:

The Family Needs Help, Too

Just as a recovering alcoholic's family needs education about the disease of alcoholism, so do the loved ones of the person who has been over-shopping or overspending. Just as the family of an alcoholic may need to attend Alanon or therapy, the same is true for those affected by the person who has been in the throes of compulsives shopping or spending.

Addiction is a family issue. Compulsive shopping and spending is a family issue. Success for the entire family rests on family members taking care of themselves and in offering the most appropriate means of support to those in need.

What does it feel like to be going through this?

_____

_____

_____

_____

_____

_____

_____

_____

What is your strategy to take care of yourself and also to support your loved one in a healthy, positive way?

1._____
2._____
3._____
4._____
5._____
6._____
7._____
8._____
9._____
10._____

Help for Those Afraid of Shopping or Spending

As we have seen, many relationships include a partner who tends to over-shop or overspend and a partner who tends to hold on too tightly to money. Each overcompensates for the other; yet, neither is balanced or healthy. As the over-shopper or overspender learns to reign in his excesses, the other partner also needs to look at letting go of the reigns a bit, too.

Sometimes it's necessary for the frugal partner to enter counseling to identify where his patterns originate and for assistance in resolving them. What I've found in my work with individual clients as well as couples is that when the frugal partner loosens his reigns, his partner's spendthrift ways subside. As arguments decrease, so do the stress, resentment, and rebellion that often fuel a bout of shopping or spending. If you can find a way to spend more time, attention and to give more appreciation to your loved one, he or she will begin to feel filled up and won't be as driven to shop or spend. Both partners play a role in recovery.

As we've also seen, money is energy and expressions of love may also come through money. Many people who feel unloved go shopping or spend money to feel love or to give love. It is likely that if you are holding onto money too tightly you are also holding back both the giving of your love and the openness to receive love from others.

What are some ways in which you can stretch yourself to loosen the reigns a bit to show your love in a modest, affordable, and healthy way? Flowers? Dinner and a movie? Tickets to a sporting event? A favorite book, Cd, or DVD?
1.
2.
3.
4.
5.

Starting a Self-Help Group

Here are some ideas I've used to start & maintain C.A.S.A.:

1. Contact Debtors Anonymous at 781-453-2743 or www.debtorsanonymous.org.
2. Establish a meeting place and time
3. Create flyers and mail, post and fax about town especially to courts, churches, counseling offices, newspapers, criminal defense attorneys, bookstores, coffee shops (include a contact phone number or e-mail)
4. Create a website
5. Post flyers at other support group meetings
6. List your group information with your state's self-help clearinghouse—usually located in your state's capital
7. Write an article (even anonymously) for a paper
8. Notify employers/businesses or employee assistance and human resources departments that may pass on the word
9. Ask for ideas or help from friends/family
10. List in your local newspaper's health calendar

List some of your ideas:

1.

2.

3.

4.

5.

6.

7.

8.

9.

10.

Epilogue

Where do we go from here?

The world stands on the brink here in the first decade of the 21st century. It seems that, at least in America, the rich have been getting richer and the poor have been getting poorer. And the middle-class has been shrinking. Will we "devolve" or regress to an "every man for himself" mentality? Will the conflict between hyper-materialism and hyper-spiritualism (West vs. East) find a middle ground?

We neither have to overindulge nor deny ourselves. It's a matter of learning balance. It's no different with food, alcohol, relationships, work, or any other aspect of life.

I believe we are smart enough individually and collectively to realize and manifest a different way.

Recovery is possible. Balance is possible. Abundance is possible. Imagine a world where this is possible. Let it begin with me... and with you.

We've got to get back to what's important. Certainly, money and life's little comforts play a part. But let's remember what else is important: our health, our relationships, our sense of purpose and meaning, our community, our environment, our spirituality.

One day at a time our sanity is restored. First we stop the bleeding—unnecessary money going down the drain. We curtail our focus on things and look around and appreciate what we do have—maybe get rid of certain possessions that are just taking up space and holding us back. If we can't do any of this, we need help and we must get that help. I'm either part of the solution or part of the problem.

Resources

The Shulman Center for Compulsive Theft & Spending
Founder/Director, Terrence Daryl Shulman, JD,LMSW

PO Box 250008 Franklin, MI 48025
Phone/Fax 248-358-8508
E-mail: terrenceshulman@theshulmancenter.com

Web sites: www.theshulmancenter.com
           www.terrenceshulman.com
           www.shopaholicsanonymous.org
           www.boughtoutandspent.com
           www.kleptomaniacsanonymous.com
           www.employeetheftsolutions.com
           www.kleptomaniacsanonymous.com
           www.somethingfornothingbook.com
           www.bitingthehandthatfeeds.com

Dr. April Benson www.stoppingovershopping.com

Debtors Anonymous www.debtorsanonymous.org

Dr. Natasha Kendal www.drsupernanny.com

Pam Landy, www.cambridgeconnection.biz

Judith Gruber, www.moneyandempowerment.com

Dr. Sally Palain, www.positiveself.net

Books

*Terrence Daryl Shulman, <u>Something for Nothing: Shoplifting Addiction and Recovery</u>, 2003

*Terrence Daryl Shulman, <u>Biting The Hand That Feeds: The Employee Theft Epidemic... New Perspectives, New Solutions</u>, 2005

*Jon E. Grant, JD, MD and S.W. Kim, MD, <u>Stop Me Because I Can't Stop Myself</u>: *Taking Control of Impulsive Behavior*, 2002

*April Benson, PhD, Editor, <u>I Shop Therefore I Am</u>, 2000

*Karen O'Connor, <u>Addicted to Shopping... and Other Issues Women Have with Money</u>, 2005

*Gloria Arenson, <u>Born to Spend: How to Overcome Compulsive Overspending</u>, 1991

*Debtors Anonymous, <u>A Currency of Hope</u>, 1999

*Julia Cameron & Mark Bryan, <u>Money Drunk, Money Sober: 90 Days to Financial Freedom</u>, 1992

*Olivia Mellon, <u>Overcoming Overspending: A Winning Plan for Spenders and Their Partners</u>, 1995

*Clarke, Daswon, & Bredehoft, <u>How Much is Enough? Everything You Need to Know to Steer Clear of Overindulging Your Children...</u>, 2003

*Paul Borthwick, <u>101 Ways to Simplify Your Life</u>, 1984

*Jenkins, Stanley, Bailey, and Markman, <u>You Paid How Much for That?</u>, 2002

*Vernon Johnson, <u>Intervention</u>, 1986

*Bert Whitehead, <u>Facing Financial Dysfunction</u>, 2002

*Rhonda Byrne, <u>The Secret</u>

*Eckhart Tolle, <u>A New Earth: Awakening to Your Life's Purpose</u>

DVDs

*<u>What Would Jesus Buy?</u>

*<u>Money as Debt</u>

*<u>From Freedom to Fascism</u>

*<u>Zeitgeist</u>

*<u>The Secret</u>

*<u>Maxed Out!</u>

Made in the USA
Columbia, SC
04 December 2023

27760763R00117